Prepare for Your Marriage

A Guidebook for Engaged Couples

Bob and Barbara Hickman

Big Oak
Publishing
Livermore, CA

Prepare for Your Marriage
A Guidebook for Engaged Couples
Copyright © 2002 by Barbara Hickman
All rights reserved.

Published by:
Big Oak Publishing
2265 Sherry Court
Livermore, CA 94550 U.S.A.

Scripture quotations are from Revised Standard Version,
American Bible Society, New York.

ISBN 0-9719653-0-7

Library of Congress Control Number: 2002091774

Publisher's Cataloging-in-Publication:
Hickman, Bob.
    Prepare for your marriage : a guidebook for engaged couples / by Bob and Barbara Hickman. — 1st ed.
    p. cm.
    Includes index.
    ISBN 0-9719653-0-7

    1. Marriage. I. Hickman, Barbara. II. Title.
HQ734.H53 2002   646.7'8
                  QBI02-200330

PRINTED IN THE UNITED STATES OF AMERICA

Acknowledgements

This manual would not have been possible without the support, advice, and assistance of many people. Among them are Art and Julie Shultz and Doug and Judy Wyatt, co-team members on our Engaged Encounter weekends, where our interest in helping engaged couples off to a good start became a fulfilling activity. Our good friend and pastor, Rev. Dr. Ken Mikulasek and dear friends Max and Marilyn Schell helped with our one-day program, One In Christ, where we hatched the idea for this guidebook, with their moral support. Pastor Ken accompanied his support with a plea for us to publish so he could share it with the couples he marries. Dan Poynter, through his book, "The Self-Publishing Manual," convinced Barb that she could actually get this information into bookstores and onto library shelves nationwide. Our friends Dave and Ada Dorn and, again, Art and Julie Shultz and Pastor Ken assisted in previewing an early manuscript draft. Graphic designers John Cole and Bob Aulicino offered their invaluable advice and counsel in the areas of both pre-press procedures and what to expect from printers. Ken Debono, of Falcon Books, continues to share his wisdom and experience in the world of book publishing, along with expertise in text design and cover design. Alex Dourouv, of Utkaduck Design, lent his creative talents in developing our web page for the website for Big Oak Publishing. We're also indebted, of course, to the many engaged couples who participated in our weekend programs for their appreciation of our efforts, and to our daughters, Beth and Brenda, who were the original inspiration. We thank all of these folks and many more for their support and encouragement in helping this book become a reality.

"A successful marriage is based on three major decisions:

1. Choose the right person.
2. Be the right person.
3. Want to stay married."

— Anonymous

Warning – Disclaimer

This book is designed to provide information in regard to the subject matter covered. It is sold with the understanding that the publisher and authors are not engaged in rendering legal advice, professional counseling, or other professional services. If legal or other expert assistance is required, the services of a competent professional should be sought.

It is not the purpose of this guidebook to reprint all the information that is otherwise available to the reader, the authors, or the publisher, but to complement, amplify, and supplement other texts. You are urged to read all the available material, learn as much as possible about marriage and marriage preparation and to tailor the information to your individual needs and circumstances.

Marriage preparation as presented in this guidebook is not a cure-all one-day exercise, but an on-going process which takes time and effort. Occasionally during this process some couples realize that they are not ready for marriage or that they no longer want to marry their intended. Other couples find validation of the suitability of their relationship for marriage. Still others find that although they are not yet ready for marriage, by following the guidelines available in this and other texts they can make the necessary adjustments. Thus, whether they eventually marry or not, most couples find this book helpful in solidifying their marriage plans.

Every effort has been made to make this guidebook as complete and accurate as possible. However, there may be mistakes, both typographical and in content. Therefore, this text should be used only as a guide and not as the ultimate source of marriage preparation information.

Prepare for Your Marriage
A Guidebook for Engaged Couples

Table of Contents

We Believe in Marriage!

— Bob and Barbara Hickman

Before You Begin ...

The real first edition of this book was written in 1989, for altruistic reasons. We knew that we had learned something very important, something vital to a lasting marriage. We'd been helping engaged couples prepare for their marriage in workshops for a number of years but we wanted to reach more couples. And we did. Now, several years later, we see that the need exists more than ever, and so we have up-dated, kept the good parts, and make it available again, this time to the general public. The institutions in our society are failing to adequately prepare people for marriage, have failed for decades. ("Sex Education" is *not* marriage preparation.) Perhaps institutions don't see it as their responsibility. And maybe it isn't. But usually parents don't prepare their offspring, clergy can only do so much in the limited time they have with couples, and most people don't know how to prepare themselves, except to follow the examples they see around them every day. Too often that example is not a lasting and fulfilling marriage, but rather a broken relationship. And it has now been demonstrated that the "divorce mentality" is self-perpetuating. We want to help put a stop to that mentality, to help people get back on track to where they really want to be.

Our Inspiration

The original manual was inspired by and based in part on our experience with Engaged Encounter, a program for couples planning to marry. The program was begun by a group in Southern California as an outgrowth of Marriage Encounter, the marriage enrichment program. We began our involvement in improving marriages in 1978 and expanded to include marriage preparation in 1979. We founded a Northern California Chapter of Engaged Encounter, and later went on to become presidents of the national organization, Lutheran Engaged Encounter of America, Inc. Recognizing that there were areas where this program needed broader coverage, we drew on additional study in sociology, and communication, plus our own growing experience, and the thoughts and ideas of approximately 50 other authors on marriage and marriage preparation to create a one-day marriage preparation program we called ONE IN CHRIST. We offered this program for a number of years, until Bob had a job relocation. Later Barb enrolled in counselor training, trained as a Prepare/Enrich counselor for married and engaged couples, continued academic communication studies (which led to an M.A. degree), and gained experience in counseling both singles and couples.

Our experience with all of these programs has been most rewarding. Time after time we've seen both married and engaged couples who were guided by our words, encouraged to confide in one another by our own openness, and inspired to make their marriage a lifetime commitment. We've also seen young couples who realized as they were going through the program that they were not ready for a lifetime commitment, or perhaps were marrying for the wrong reasons, and decided to either postpone or maybe even cancel their wedding plans. While that is not a happy time, in our experience it has always been a mutual decision, and we've never heard any regrets. We, and the many others who have worked with us, have helped countless engaged couples, and married couples, too, learn the basic principles needed to make a marriage last a lifetime, and learn how to apply them to their own lives.

We Want To Make It Clear...

We did not *create* these principles. In fact, we learned some of them on our first Marriage Encounter weekend, after 20 years of marriage! But we realized that we'd been living them all along – we just didn't know what it was that we were doing so right! The best thing about these principles is that they do not become outmoded. (Compare that with a computer manual!) They are as sound today as when they were first developed. All we have to do is apply them.

Though we have indeed helped many couples learn about marriage and what makes it work, we are well aware of the many other couples who do not attend the programs or receive counseling – those who can't afford either the time or the money; those who live in an area where nothing is offered; those who aren't aware that such help is available; even those who think they know all they need to know. This book is aimed at any couple who seeks guidance.

We Also Want To Make It Clear...

Although Barb has had training and experience in family counseling, in marriage enrichment and premarital counseling, and has a post-graduate degree in communication, this book is not intended to be a substitute for pastoral counseling or parents' advice. And it's not meant to be a substitute for the weekend experience that the text is modeled after. It is a guide that has been created and designed for those who wish to supplement the professional counseling that is available to them.

We hope that many couples discover this guidebook and will use it; that clergy will offer it as a complement to the very important and personal pastoral counseling; that parents will give it to their sons and daughters and their friends' sons and daughters; that engaged couples will give it to their friends. **We believe in marriage**, and it is our hope that every engaged couple have the opportunity to learn, from the beginning, how they can make their marriage the best it can be, fulfilling and rewarding to both husband and wife for as long as they both shall live.

– Bob and Barbara Hickman
Livermore, California

"There is no more lovely, friendly, and charming relationship than a good marriage."

– Martin Luther

1

Here We Go!

How to Use this Book

Before we get into the explanation of how to use this guidebook, please take a moment right how to reflect on why you're doing this. Did your parents or maybe your clergyman, or even your fiancé pressure you into it? Did a friend recommend it? Are you concerned that maybe you aren't ready for marriage yet and want to find out? Or are you sure about your choice of mate and just want to get the best foundation that you can as you begin your new life together? Whatever the reason, we ask that you go through the exercises with an open mind, accepting the suggestions, the questions and the answers you give and get, as gifts of love from whomever they were offered. You can be sure that whoever recommended this book cares about you and wants the best for you and your marriage.

Our Purpose

The purpose of this book is to encourage the two of you to take the time to prepare for your marriage – not your wedding, but your marriage – and to give you the guidance that will help you develop a firm foundation, one that's right for *your* relationship. But don't expect a miracle. We're not ultimate authorities, with all the answers.

We don't have a magic formula for "living happily ever after." We have proven principles to pass along to you and if you apply these principles, well, good things will happen. We'll share with you our lives and what we've learned. We'll probably cover subjects that some of you have already discussed and maybe even settled. Our experiences and background are different from yours. Maybe you're going into a second marriage; maybe you plan to have a two-career family; surely there are other differences. What we'll do is relate proven principles of successful marriages, along with methods of handling various situations, then show how we applied them to our situation. Your lives won't be our lives, but in truth, all we can offer to our partner in marriage is our real selves. And that's what this is all about – discovering your real selves, then sharing it with each other.

The Process

The information presented in this guidebook is a package deal. To skip any part of it is an enormous loss. Each successive exercise builds on the previous ones, so it's important to read them in the order given and to complete each one before going on to the next. You'll find that each section deals with a different topic. After reading the text together, take time *right then* to reflect on how the information given in the text applies to you and your relationship. Read it again if necessary. You'll find helpful suggestions and questions (based on ideas used in questions from Engaged Encounter) at the end of each section to help you with this reflection. We recommend that you each write down your thoughts in spiral notebooks which you purchase especially for this purpose, one for each of you. It's best to go into separate rooms when you write so that what or how much you write is not influenced by what your partner is doing; each should have privacy during the writing time.

When you put your thoughts down on paper it's very important to be open and honest with yourself, and with one another. Please don't conceal true opinions to spare yourself or your fiancé embarrassment or disappointment. The truth comes out as marriages develop anyway. By being honest in the beginning, you'll build the foundation for trust in the future. You can write personally and confidently, with the knowledge that what you write is for your fiancé only – no one else will be reading your notebooks. Write your name on it and mark it "PRIVATE!."

Please resist the temptation to skip the writing and go straight into a discussion on any of these topics. We've found that both of us are far more open and revealing of our inner selves when we take the time to write than when we only speak to each other. When writing, we're able to concentrate more fully on our own thoughts without the distraction of someone else talking and the concern of having a response ready. As Barb says, "When I write I can say all that I have to say before Bob changes the subject or interrupts with his own response." And Bob says that he can get all his thoughts on paper before Barb's expression tells him that she has something more important to say to him. To get the most benefit from each exercise, do **write** your answers to the questions first, before moving on to the discussion.

As you write, keep in mind that penmanship, spelling, punctuation, and grammar aren't important here. You're writing to your beloved, one who already accepts you as you are. Ideas, feelings, hopes, dreams, and opinions are what we bring to our marriage, and those **are** important. We also recommend that you respond fully, even if you think your fiancé already knows the answer. We've seen more than one couple who both believed that an issue was settled, then later realized that each thought the other had agreed to his or her different way! Of course, they had to begin all over again.

After the time for writing is over, get back together and exchange your notebooks with each other, making no comments, positive or negative. Each of you then read what the other has lovingly written for you, reading with love and acceptance. Following this, take time to discuss the topic and what each of you has written. Because you love one another, this discussion, too, should be open, candid, and loving. Be open to what your fiancé has to say, accepting his/her views as a true expression of who he/she is. It isn't necessary to be in full agreement in order to accept another's feelings as both real and legitimate. Love is the key.

But First You'll Need to...

The process is as simple as that. But before you begin, you'll need to provide that spiral notebook and a pen or pencil for each of you, and have access to a timer. Then you'd be wise to decide on a schedule for completing the exercises at the end of each chapter. You might want to do one or two sections each night for a week, or maybe do half on one Saturday, half the next. Working on this just one night each week is the least effective. With six days between sessions, much of the fringe information has been forgotten and the building-on-the-previous-exercise advantage is lost. It's best to cover the whole book in as compact a time-frame as possible, being careful to allow the full time suggested for each topic.

Whichever schedule you choose, we urge you to cover the topics in the order given. The text for each is based on the previous sections; the later information will make better sense and be more beneficial and more meaningful if you've completed the earlier topics first.

If you've thumbed through the book already, you've probably noticed that each section consists of text explaining the topic, followed by a number of leading sentences or questions for you to reflect on, with a suggested minimum time for writing and discussion. (You might want to photocopy these pages, making one copy for each of you.) Using these suggestions as a guide for your reflection, write until you hear the timer signal to stop. If you finish before the time is up, go back and see if maybe you rushed through the exercise too fast, skipped some, or maybe you can elaborate on one or two of your answers. If you haven't finished when the time signals, ask for another few minutes, until you can get all your thoughts down on paper.

When you're both finished writing, get together and exchange notebooks, each reading what your fiancé has written. Then set the timer for the minimum discussion time and orally exchange the thoughts and feelings inspired by your fiancé's writing. Take as much time as you need for discussion, but if you finish before the timer sounds, you're perhaps rushing through or glossing over something important; maybe you need to re-read your notebooks or the questions. When you reach the end of your discussion, take a short break before going on to the next section. So, that's:

1. Read the chapter together.
2. Each take a notebook and a pen (and a copy of the questions).
3. Set the timer for the time suggested.
4. Separate to write.
5. Get together and exchange notebooks.
6. Discuss what was written, for the suggested amount of time.
7. Take a short break, then start on the next chapter.

Final Hints

As you work through these exercises, keep in mind that, just as a marriage takes two to make it work, any marriage preparation will help only if you both work with it. When one person opens up and reveals himself or herself, and the other doesn't, it can be very hurtful. In an exercise like this, both need to be open and honest to get the most out of this time together, and start building a bond of trust.

Another thing to be aware of is that we often convince ourselves that "if it's what he/she wants, then it's what I want." That's okay in many instances; compromise and sacrifice are a part of any marriage. But for our purposes during these exercises, you need to think first about your own wants and needs. Make sure that your answers are truly your own, and make sure that it's not just what you think your fiancé wants to hear. To give you an example, as we sat down to dinner one evening during our 15th year of marriage or so, one of our daughters complained that "we're having spinach again!" Being a conscientious mother, Barb explained that spinach is very nutritious and, besides, "your father likes spinach." Bob smiled and said, "That's right, except that it's your mother who likes spinach." We learned then, after those many years of eating frozen spinach at least once a week, that neither of us likes frozen spinach, yet we each thought the other did! So be sure to verify within your own mind that the responses you give to the questions are your own.

This is Our Story

One more thing before you get started. Well, two more things, and both are important for you to know. First, realize that Barb was a stay-at-home Mom as our children were growing up. Since many couples these days choose to be a two-career family, there will be some differences between our situation and how we worked things out and your situation and how you work things out. The principles remain the same; it's the application of those principles that will be different.

The second important thing for you to know is that both of us grew up with religion as a part of our lives; we've both been active in the Lutheran church since early childhood. You'll be reading about how our faith and our Christianity has affected our lives and our relationship. But we know that not many readers of this book have the same background, so we've tried to make it as universally acceptable as we can, while not denying our true selves, and still make our point. We believe that a good marriage is important to everyone, regardless of religious background, and we want to be able to help everyone who has chosen this book as their guide. So we ask your indulgence if we seem to you to "go overboard." For example, to us it's very natural to begin a project like this with a prayer. If you're comfortable with prayer, now is a good time to use it. If prayer is foreign to you, and you'd rather skip it, that's okay. (But if you'd like to try it, now is a good time to start.)

Since this is a time to focus on each other and your relationship, we suggest that you hold your fiancé's hand, close your eyes and each take a turn audibly thanking God for some special quality about your beloved that seems very prominent at the moment. For example, sometimes Barb thinks that Bob's most endearing quality is his thoughtfulness, other times his tenderness. Bob says that Barb's may be her determination to carry a project through to success, or maybe that day it's her devotion to our family. The particular quality we choose will change, of course, depending on what's going on in our lives at the time. Right now, won't you please take a moment to think about your fiancé's goodness? At first you might be more comfortable with a silent prayer, but we encourage you to say it aloud, so that your fiancé **knows** what you think is special about him/her. Done with love and confidence before each session, this simple practice can set the mood for the success of your work.

Now you're ready to begin, guidebook in hand, spiral notebooks, pens, and timer nearby. Used properly, this book will help you learn that good marriages don't just happen – they must be developed. That takes time and effort, but it's worth it. Remember the phrase that we've heard from a number of sources and is the motto of Engaged Encounter: "A wedding is just a day, but a marriage is a lifetime." We agree.

Reflection #1

(Suggested minimum time for writing,
10 minutes; discussion, 10 minutes)

For your first reflection, you can just write the following in your note-book:

- The reason I am doing this preparation for our marriage is because…
- What I hope to gain is…

(Your mind might be a little fuzzy as to why you're doing this and what you expect to get out of it, but you must have some thoughts about it. Write them down. Then lovingly share them with your fiancé.)

2

Hey! I'm O.K.!

Getting to Really Know Yourself

"Know thyself" is a great admonition. Do *you* know who you are? Or *what* you are? Most of us don't, unless we've actually sat down and thought about it. But if you don't know who and what you are, how can you be ready to share yourself in marriage? The Bible urges us to love our neighbor as ourselves (Matthew 22:39). Those words tell us that we can't truly love and accept another unless we *do* accept ourselves. We're going to ask you to learn who you are so that when you share yourself, both you and your fiancé know what is being offered. We also have to love and care about ourselves and respect ourselves so that we understand what love and care and respect are. These things build on each other; we can't love another unless we fully love ourselves; and we can't love ourselves unless we accept who we really are. So we'll begin by helping you find out who you really are.

My Images

Finding out who you are isn't easy. It takes real courage to honestly face ourselves. But, again, unless we're honest with ourselves we won't be honest with anyone else. However, the real person that we call "me" is sometimes hard to identify because, sometimes, we hide behind an "image" that we want people to see. Barb gives a simple example:

> I'm a good homemaker. At least, I like to think I am, and I want other people to think so, too. So, for instance, when I have to serve store-bought cookies instead of homemade ones, I make sure that everyone understands why they aren't homemade. Or if the house happens to be a mess when the doorbell rings, I probably won't invite the guest in – I don't want to spoil the "good homemaker" image, even when it isn't quite accurate.

Note that an image isn't necessarily phony, although it might be sometimes, or maybe for some people it is all the time. When we hide behind the image, we probably do it because we're afraid that people won't like us as well or that we'll disappoint them if they find out the real truth. So we present a "public image."

Another kind of image that we all have is the one that other people see in us, an image that we may or may not intentionally project. We can tell what they think of us from the feedback that we get in the form of compliments and criticism. We also get non-verbal messages in their eyes, voices, and behavior toward us. Sometimes we agree with their image of us, such as when they give a compliment on something we're proud of. Other times we disagree, such as when we know we wouldn't have gotten that compliment if they knew the real truth. Again Barb gives an example:

> A while back when we square danced every week, one of the ladies complimented me on my tiny waistline (okay, it was a *long* while back). Outwardly I gave the proper, "Thank you," but inwardly I wondered if she was aware of the rolls of fat hiding under my belt. Maybe she *was* aware, and decided that I looked nice anyway.

So which image was correct – the one the friend complimented, or the one Barb knew was there?

In addition to the images we purposely project for others to see and the image of us that others perceive, we have our personal perception of ourselves, our own self-image. Have you ever taken the time to just sit down and think about you? What do you like about yourself? What do you dislike? Right now, each of you get your notebooks and pens, set the timer for 2 minutes, turn your backs to each other (so you'll have a bit of privacy) and make a list of your strengths, your strong points, the things you like about yourself. Then set the timer again for 2 minutes and make a second list, this time writing down your weaknesses, things you could improve, the things you dislike about yourself. Do it right now.

Time Out!

Was that easy? Or was it difficult to come up with more than just a few items on your list? An exercise like this helps you to get in touch with what and who you are, and gives you direction for the future. If you don't like what you wrote, you can work to improve it; if you do like what you see on the paper, you know that you're on the right track toward the kind of person you want to be.

Most people have times when their self-image is good. These are times when they appreciate and enjoy their own talents and good qualities. But other times our self-image isn't very good. We magnify our weaknesses, compare ourselves to others and see ourselves as inferior. Or we use a double standard by forgiving another person's mistake but stay angry at ourselves for the same mistake. We probably *all* do this; it's part of human nature, part of the ups and downs of life.

The <u>Real</u> "Me"

Now you can see why, with these various images we all have, it's very hard to identify the *real* person so that we can accept and love the real person that we each are. It's especially difficult to love ourselves when we know that we sometimes project an image to others that isn't accurate or we get compliments that we think we don't deserve. Or we get criticism that we know we do deserve. So how can we tell which of these is the *real* person? We'll tell you how (this is another thing we've learned). In Bob's words:

> The real me is the person I let others see, *and* it's what others think of me, *and* it's how I see myself – it's a combination of these, and more. That's because the *real* me is the unique person God created. Now, to carry this further, we know that everything God made is *good*! The Bible tells us that. So, the real me is the most lovable of all of these because the real me is what God created!

Bob is right. In Genesis 1:31 we read "God saw all that He had made, and it was very good." Since He had already created man (in Genesis 1:27) this means that even with our faults (real or not), every one of us *must* be basically good, and therefore lovable, because *God* made each one of us. Of course, because we sin we've all picked up blemishes along the way, those things we try to hide from others. But underneath those blemishes that we sometimes hide behind a public image, there is a good person. And despite those blemishes, those weaknesses and inadequacies, God loves us, each one of us. Bob continues:

> Knowing that God loves me, faults and weaknesses and all, helps me to accept myself, faults and all. If He can love me, then I guess I can love me, too. Knowing this helps me to accept other people's faults, too. God loves them, so I should, too. When I truly accept others, I can love them more fully. That includes Barb.

The complete honesty with ourselves mentioned earlier extends to our mate when marriage enters the picture. We need to allow ourselves to be vulnerable and to honestly share our *true* self with our spouse, not some perfect image we want him or her to love, and not an idealized image that he or she wants to see.

It's a little scary to admit to some feelings, such as fears, frustrations, and embarrassments, and accept them as a part of ourselves. Maybe we're afraid that what we're feeling is somehow wrong? Well, there's no such thing as a "wrong" feeling – or a "right" feeling. Feelings are spontaneous reactions within us; we can't control them. We can control our *behavior* in response to feelings, but we can't control the feeling itself. So, the feeling can't be right or wrong; it just happens.

But as natural and spontaneous as they may be, revealing these feelings to another person is even scarier than admitting them to ourselves, because it makes us vulnerable. Most of us are more comfortable when we hide those aspects of ourselves from other people. However, Barb is willing to admit:

> I cry easily when I see a touching scene. Sometimes at wed-
> dings, and once at a baptism, when a whole family was bap-
> tized, parents and three children. Movies, too, can cause tears
> to well up sometimes. Like many people, when this happens I try
> to hide it because I'm a little embarrassed by it. But when I let
> Bob see this intimate part of me, and he accepts it lovingly, with-
> out criticism or ridicule, a bond of trust develops between us. He
> has experienced a very private part of me, and hasn't rejected
> me, so it's easier to allow myself to become vulnerable in the fu-
> ture, in other situations. I'm willing to let him see more of the real
> me, rather than hiding behind an image I've chosen.

SUMMARY

We hope that you now understand that you must love, respect, and fully accept yourself before you can truly love and respect and accept another person, including your fiancé. The major points in accepting yourself:

- Learn what is truly there: learn by identifying the images you project, the images others see in you, and your self-image.
- Realize that the *real* person, the one behind those images, is the **best** one because that's the unique person that God created.
- If God still loves you, with all the faults and blemishes you've developed over the years (and he *does*), surely you can love yourself.

When you love and accept yourself, you can more fully love and accept others. And when you allow your fiancé to see the true person, rather than just an image, you can be sure that he/she loves the real person, and not just the image. And it's the *real* person who will be married.

Now it's time for your reflection on all of this. You'll find guidelines on the next page. (Don't forget, you can photocopy them so you'll have a copy for each of you.) Remember to set the timer for the minimum writing time, separate to write, then write until you hear the signal to stop.

Since this is a "self" reflection, you won't be exchanging notebooks this time. So remember as you write that this is for your own knowledge. This one time you are writing just for yourself; you can be truly open and accepting. (You can exchange with your fiancé later, if you choose to, but for now, it's just for you.) When you hear the signal to stop, just return to your fiancé for a short break before starting on the next topic.

Reflection #2

(Suggested minimum writing time,
15 minutes; no discussion time)

(There may be too many points here for you to respond to in the time allowed, so don't feel badly if you don't finish them all – just ask for more time. Write on each as completely as you can before going on to the next.)

- Who am I?
    - a. The specific qualities I want others to see in me include…
    - b. Judging by compliments and feedback I get, others see me as…
    - c. What is my self-image?
       What do I like about myself? …dislike?
- When I read this description I feel…
- I see some things in myself that may make it difficult to love me, such as…
- The best qualities that I am bringing to our marriage are…
- How has my view of myself changed since I met him/her?
- I feel (comfortable/uncomfortable) telling him/her my deepest thoughts and feelings because…

"To Love Is A Decision"

— Anonymous

3

I'll Take Romance!
The Cycles in Marriage

Most of us realize that a successful marriage takes more than "being in love." For one thing, it takes understanding – of the marriage relationship. Love is a part of it, of course. But married love isn't always constant.

We've learned that there are phases of love that constantly re-occur throughout a marriage. These phases of love go through a cycle, of sorts. Maybe rollercoaster is a better description some-times. Just as everyone has ups and downs in their lives, so does a marriage. In fact, the up and down cycle can apply to many things – a job, a vacation, a book you read, or even a purchase you've made. We experienced that when we bought a car recently, a used car. It seemed to be just what we wanted; the right size, had all the fea-tures we wanted, it seemed almost perfect for us. The price was less than we expected, and Bob was able to bargain for an even lower price. We had found a real gem. But now that we've had it a while, we notice that the gas mileage isn't as good as we expected it to be, and the interior isn't as clean as it first appeared to be, and the color isn't what we would have chosen. It's still a good car, and we like it, but it isn't as near perfect as we first thought it was. That kind of thing can happen in a marriage, too. In the beginning it seems *so* good. Then after a while...

The First Phase

We both like what we call the "romance" phase of this cycle in marriage; it's the "up" part. Like most young couples, during our dating days we focused on the good in our relationship, those meaningful little things that we liked to share; we were oblivious to anything that would cause irritation between us. It was a very romantic time, a time when we focused on each other. It didn't matter what we did or where we went, just being together made the occasion special. Simple things brought us the most pleasure; we went on walks, picnics, anything that was low cost! Barb remembers:

> Bob was away at school during part of that time, and I wrote to him every day, sometimes a note, sometimes a poem. His letters always made me feel special and loved. I was so anxious to join him on campus. I wanted to share his life at school and meet his friends. I wanted to learn the things that he enjoyed, so we went horseback-riding. (Just once, but I went!) And I was eager for him to enjoy the things that I liked, so we went roller skating. (That didn't happen very often either.) He tried it simply because I enjoyed it.

> After almost every date, we'd sit and talk for what seemed like hours, about anything and everything. It was so romantic. We continued to have those long conversations when Bob came home from work, and even now that he's retired. We sit down, maybe have a glass of wine, and talk about the events of the day or anything else that pops into our heads.

These on-going little bits of romance in our lives, then and now, help us to focus on each other. They keep us from being self-centered, making him/her the center of our attention. When you think about it, that's what romance is, focusing your attention and your thoughts on your beloved. Barb continues:

During dating I let him know how much I appreciated many of his traits, such as his control of anger, and how I enjoyed not having to share him with sports, even on TV. (He's never been an avid athlete, and I was grateful for that!) I tried to please him in every way I could. I even wore a dress I didn't like – it was the wrong color, bad style, didn't fit. But I wore it anyway, simply because he liked it.

And from Bob's viewpoint:

Barb and I met at the local grocery store. She worked in the produce department and was a checker, and I was a stock boy and bagger. So, without even trying, we were able to see each other several times a week. When we began dating, our joys came from simple pleasures and doing special things for each other. Once for her birthday, when I lived a hundred miles away at school, I bought her a black-raspberry milkshake, packed it in dry ice, carried it for two hours on a Greyhound bus, then hitch-hiked the last 10 miles to her home. The look of delight on her face when she saw the container made it all worthwhile – with neither of us saying a word, she knew what effort I had gone through to get it to her. I still bring her an occasional box of her favorite candy, but nothing can match that black-raspberry milkshake.

I loved our long talks in those days. We learned a lot about each other, and our friendship deepened. During college days, on Sunday afternoons we would go for a walk or, if the weather was bad, we'd hold hands and read the comics together. And we *still* read the Sunday paper together.

While we were dating, Barb always looked nice and smelled good. I always wanted to look my best for her, too, so I'd shower and shave before our dates. Over the years many things have changed, but I still shower and shave at night so that I'll smell nice and feel good to her when we go to bed together. After almost 45 years of marriage, I *still* want to please her.

When we focus on each other, we want to *do* things for the other – Barb will maybe help with the yard work, or clean up the garage, or paint a wall; Bob might give top priority to a project Barb has asked him to do, or bring home a special present. When either of us does this sort of thing, the other knows that he/she is in the romance phase of the cycle.

The Second Phase

When there's an "up" phase, you know there *has* to be a "down" phase (otherwise the "up" wouldn't be up!) We call this "disillusionment." These "down" periods are like potholes in the road of life. Things will be going along smoothly, then – BONK! – a pothole! Disappointment in your spouse, or in marriage, or expectations that aren't met – any of these can bring on disillusionment. Even something that seemed so good before marriage can turn into a problem. Bob remembers:

> One thing I liked while we were dating was Barb's enjoyment of children. She really loved to care for and play with her nephews and nieces – we both did. But after we married, I noticed that the more she did for them, the less time she had for *me*. Another thing, Barb always looked great on our dates; after our wedding I found out how much time she spent on looking good. Fellows, do you know how *long* it can take your fiancé to get ready to go somewhere?!
>
> I don't know what I had expected, but this wasn't it! At times I lost sight of Barb's wants and needs and was only concerned about myself. That hadn't happened much during our dating days; then I was centered on *her*.

Periods of disillusionment can be as short as a few minutes, or sometimes they hang around for weeks or more. It still happens for each of us, even after many years of marriage. Sometimes it's caused by a disappointment or maybe when we expected something that didn't happen. It doesn't require an argument or something else obvious. One of us might not even know that the other is feeling disillusionment. It's the *attitude* that causes the problem for most of us; our focus has shifted from the *person* to something he or she has said or done – or maybe something *not* said or done. Instead of looking for ways to express love, an attitude of self-centeredness causes us to look for ways that our beloved *doesn't* measure up. This can bring on feelings of sadness, loneliness, and we may even feel sorry for ourselves. That's disillusionment.

An example from Barb:

> I mentioned earlier that during our courtship I felt very lucky that Bob was not a sports fan. I was so smug, knowing that I would never be a "football widow" or a "golf widow." *Our* life wouldn't be like that.
>
> Then we learned to play tennis. I loved it right from the start. I took lessons, joined a league, entered tournaments – the whole bit. But Bob, was not interested in sports, so he didn't like it as much as I did. I wanted him to share my exciting experiences. He didn't. I had to enjoy them alone. Looking back on it, I think I was disappointed that he didn't try harder to please me.

And another example, from Barb:

> During our dating days, we rarely quarreled or even disagreed. Bob was so easy to get along with. He never got angry or upset about anything. After we married, I realized that he's just as patient with others, but I didn't like it! *He* hadn't changed. *I* just hadn't faced reality until after we married. I *wanted* him to be angry about the moving van that was late, and about the contractor who wouldn't build our house the way we wanted it. I'm still disappointed when he remains calm while I'm so upset. I feel lonely, like I'm fighting the battles alone, that I'm the only one who cares. I should be *proud* of him and his even temper, but there are times I want him to do things *my* way.
>
> Like everyone else, when I become self-centered, I put *my* wants and needs and preferences before Bob's. I'm no longer Bob-centered, and disillusionment sets in.

Yes, disillusionments still occur for us. During a recent Christmas season we decided to finally build a stable for the little nativity set we've had for years. As Bob tells it:

> Barb drew up a rough design and I went out and bought the materials so I could make it. It was cold working in the garage, but the thought of finally having this project completed kept me going. When I brought the finished product in to show Barb, I was pretty proud of it, even though it wasn't quite as polished-looking as the store-bought kind.
>
> But Barb's reaction was disappointing to me. Instead of admiring it and telling me how nice it looked, as I expected her to, she said, "Is that it?! Is it finished?" The wave of sadness that disillusionment brings came over me. And probably the same thing happened to Barb when she first saw it. She was obviously expecting something quite different.

To make a longer story short, we agreed that the "stable" would make a nice birdfeeder for our back yard. So you see, it still happens to us; it isn't just a phenomenon of early marriage.

A BIG Decision

So what can we do about it? Well, another important thing that we've learned over the years is that long-lasting love is not just a feeling, an emotion that emerges when we're near our beloved. Feelings and emotions can come and go quite rapidly and, as we pointed out earlier, we can't control feelings. You know yourself that you can feel happy as a lark as you get out of bed, and then feel stress or anger after you've read the newspaper, and your whole mood is different. Obviously, emotions are too changeable and too undependable to be the only basis for a life-long relationship like marriage. This means that love for a husband or wife must be based on something more stable and more durable than an emotion, if it's going to last a lifetime.

To love or to be loved is more than just a feeling. It's a **decision**, especially in marriage. Deciding to love is a choice we make. The emotional feeling of love is the manifestation, an expression of the decision to love. While we don't have control over our feelings, we do have control over our relationship and our actions, and so do you with your fiancé, by deciding to love. We can control our relationship, and the direction it is headed, with a conscious decision.

Making the decision to love can lead away from disillusionment. We could leave our relationship in disillusionment, accept it as a failure and be unhappy, or we can choose to do something about it. Neither of us will meet the other's expectations or ideals all the time, but we **decide** to accept each other. We officially made the decision to love each other for a lifetime on our wedding day and we each need to remind ourselves of that decision at times of disillusionment. It helps us to redirect our focus. Barb points out that:

> Bob *is* easy to get along with, but he doesn't always live up to my expectations. In the evening when he falls asleep on the family room floor, I might feel angry and resentful because he isn't giving me his attention. But I can *choose* to be loving and understanding, to be sensitive to his need for rest. When he turns the sprinkler on my freshly-washed windows, I might feel anger and exasperation. But I can remind myself again that our marriage is more important than spotless windows. When Bob opens the wrong side of the milk carton, or leaves his dirty socks in the living room, I need to remember that our marriage, our relationship, is more important than my teaching him to open the milk carton *my* way.

Bob has experienced this, too:

> I remember a time when I was disappointed that Barb fixed canned soup with tossed salad for supper. I had expected something more elaborate. It wasn't until I focused on Barb and her reasons for choosing that menu that I quit feeling sorry for myself.

I've decided to love Barb at all times, not just when she is at her best, or when I'm at my lovingest, but at all times. I love her when she forgets to get gas in the car, when she is discouraged about some project she is working on, and when she is too tired at night to be my lover.

This decision to love is an important part of our relationship. And the opposite side of the coin is deciding to *accept* love, even when you know you're less for him/her than you could or maybe should be. Bob tells us:

One of my short-comings is that I'm absent-minded at times. I've been known to put a dirty plate into the refrigerator then put the leftovers into the dishwasher, or maybe peel an orange and throw it into the garbage, saving the peel! When this sort of thing happens, and Barb laughingly reminds me of what I was doing, I can take her words as a criticism or take them as a help. That is, I can reject her love or I can accept it.

As we move out of disillusionment because of the decision to love, or to be loved, there are some obvious signs, usually changes in behavior. Bob tells his experience:

I become more aware of and more sensitive to Barb's needs. I listen more carefully and respond to her more positively. I can be tenderhearted and forgiving. Some people, especially men, might think this is a sign of weakness, but I think quite the contrary is true. I consider it to be a sign of emotional maturity and strength, and a sign of my love for Barb.

If we're feeling resentment as we make this decision to love, it's a signal that we're not being honest about it. This can happen when the decision is insincere, sometimes when the decision is necessary repeatedly within a short time span. But *any* kind of resentment means that we're being self-centered again. Resentment signals a need to discuss, or maybe a need for self-examination of attitudes.

The Third Phase

The decision to love leads us away from the self-pity and loneliness that is so typical of disillusionment in marriage. You might think that the natural result is an immediate return to romance. Sometimes that happens. It turns out, though, that an experience much deeper and richer can result: the **joy** of truly loving. By setting aside self-centeredness and putting each other first again, we're led to face the reality of our relationship and the beginning of a deep joy. In doing this, we're willfully giving our relationship priority over our own selfishness. Bob confides:

> Of course, in our numerous years together, I've experienced the joy that comes from loving Barb and being loved by her many, many times. I experienced it some months ago when we told each other, in love letters, why we wanted to go on living with each other. As we each read the other's words, it brought tears of deep happiness to our eyes, and not a word more needed to be spoken as we held one another in our arms. We both experienced a sense of wholeness, contentment, and peace knowing that the bottom line, no matter what, is that we both want to be married to each other forever. That's *real* joy!

This instance was a time we had a shared joy, but that isn't always the case. In fact, often we can go through this cycle alone or be at a different stage of the cycle from the other.

SUMMARY

In marriage we need to be honest and open and accepting not only with ourselves but also with our husband or wife, and allow ourselves to be vulnerable so that our friendship can deepen into intimacy. It's important to recognize the phases of love in a marriage relationship:

- Romance: what we want to be there, *all* the time.
- Disillusionment: the loneliness we feel when things don't go as we expected because we've shifted our focus from our beloved.

- Joy: the deep, rich feeling that sometimes comes after disillusionment, when we put aside our self-centeredness.

It should now be very clear that we can't rely on feelings alone. Feelings are too changeable to form the sole basis of a life-long relationship. It should also be clear that long-lasting love overlooks imperfections, unmet expectations, and disappointment. Long-lasting love includes making a conscious decision to love, then making it again, and again – as many times as necessary.

Now for the reflection and writing. Again, we encourage you to respond to every item even if your fiancé already knows what you will say. Couples sometimes discover that they've had a misunderstanding and this is a perfect opportunity to straighten it out. Other times they confirm their understanding of each other. Either result is good.

Reflection #3

(15 minutes minimum for writing,
10 minutes minimum for discussion)

- Sometimes I think you don't accept me as I am because …
- I think maybe you would like me to be different from what I am when…
- Some of the little things I like to do for you are…
- Some of the little things I like that you do for me are…
- A time when I experienced disillusionment in our relationship was…
- When we're first married I expect that you'll be disillusioned by…
- One time when I made a decision to love you was…
- A time when I made a decision to accept your love was…

"A successful marriage
requires falling in love many
times — with the same person."

— Anonymous

4

We've Got to Talk!

Openness in Communication

Before we go on, we'd like to remind you of some of the pointers we gave you earlier. We encourage you to read through this guidebook together, rather than each doing it whenever you can fit it in. We also recommend that you read each chapter through completely and write on your reflection in one sitting, with no breaks. You'll find that your time spent will be more productive if you wait until the end before heading for the cookie jar.

Another very important hint is to remember to set your timer, then to write until you hear the signal to stop. Occasionally you'll be sitting there wondering what else to say, but wait just a minute and other thoughts will probably pop into your head – and it just might be your best thought of the day! And also discuss until you hear the signal to stop, even if you think you've said all that you can say about the topic. Again, some thoughts take longer to come to the surface than others.

Now, in this section we want to foster more open communication and we'll show why that's important and how openness has helped us develop and deepen our intimacy. Many couples have told us that this information and the next section have been the most helpful to them, so do read carefully; don't rush through just to get it done.

What Is Openness?

Let's start with a definition of openness. By "openness" here, we mean an absence of secrecy, complete truthfulness between the two of us, a process of talking and listening that involves elements of risk, vulnerability, trust, and acceptance. This goes beyond surface feelings, on to reactions, ideas. It includes seeing and hearing what we say with our eyes and actions, the unspoken messages. This openness reveals *all* our sensitivities, not just our faults, fears, or weak points. It also reveals our strengths and our vulnerability, particularly in the area of needs, such as our need for love and affection and our need to express love. We often hesitate to let others know of our emotional or psychological needs, even though we all have them.

This kind of openness is based on trust which deepens from a continued sharing between us. As Barb tells us:

> It comes from believing in my own goodness and in Bob's, and from trusting that he loves and accepts me with my limitations. It comes from trusting that he'll keep private the confidences revealed between the two of us, and from my being worthy of his trust.

We need to work on developing trust continually because we're growing and changing constantly. There's always something new to talk about and to build trust with. Barb continues:

> Like most wives, I find it fairly easy to talk about my surface feelings and thoughts with my husband, such as the time friends called at the last minute to cancel a dinner date. I was disappointed and angry and I didn't mind saying so. But, because we have developed an intimacy, I was also able to bring out the deeper feelings and thoughts, the hurt and the loneliness that comes from rejection. I feel comfortable telling Bob my deeper feelings because I trust him to love me and accept me as I am, and I know that he won't tell others.

Openness here doesn't mean bluntness, or to be unnecessarily hurtful. It's important to be sensitive to each other's feelings. As Bob has learned:

> Barb is an accomplished seamstress and has often made clothes for herself and our family. When she asks me how I like the new outfit and I don't, certainly it would be insensitive to her feelings to say it's ugly. It's far more loving, just as truthful, but not so blunt, to say that it's well-made but that I think another one she made was a more becoming style or color.

It requires patience to be truly open. As individuals and as males and females, we're so different that when one says something, the other can easily misunderstand or misinterpret the meaning completely. It's almost as if we are conditioned from childhood to misunderstand one another. So, often we need to clarify. Bob continues:

> Barb could easily have jumped to the conclusion that my comment about not liking the garment she made was really saying that she has bad taste in clothes, or that she can't sew well at all. And of course that isn't what I meant. What I meant was that I didn't like that one particular thing.

Even our memories of discussions or events can be totally different from each other because we each experience things from a different viewpoint, coming from different backgrounds as we do. We simply see and hear some things differently. So openness requires the patience to help each of us see things from the other's point of view. Easier said than done, of course, but we try.

Openness also requires the confidence that comes from believing in ourselves, and accepting our own strengths and weaknesses, our own good points and bad points. Bob has realized:

> I need to remember that, although I'm far from perfect, I'm basically a good person – people do love me as I really am. Barb certainly does. Knowing this, it's easier to trust her and risk vulnerability.

We're not talking here about an openness that requires revealing serious past sins during these exercises. Reveal only what's in your heart *right now*. If you feel a need to talk about past sin, you probably *should* talk about it, but contact a trusted clergy or Christian counselor before you burden your fiancé. He or she can advise if you *should* tell your beloved. If necessary, you can always ask a local church for a reference.

Be Prepared for Obstacles to Openness

This openness and trust isn't always easy, of course, and it helps to be aware of some of the obstacles we might run up against. As you might expect, there's a risk involved in being truthful. Sometimes we might not want to take that risk, so we deliberately hide things. We may have a fear of looking foolish, being misunderstood, being rejected, being wrong, being embarrassed, or even fear of losing him or her. That's pretty serious. We might not want to risk sharing dreams, beliefs, values, or goals in life, because we fear they might be "different," or seem far-fetched or unrealistic to someone else. We might not want to risk sharing deep feelings about our relationship with our parents, or our attitude about sex or about money, because it seems too personal; we want to keep part of ourselves private.

Or just the opposite, we might not want to bother to share things that seem unimportant or insignificant. But our judgment can be biased, and we often convince ourselves that something is insignificant when it really isn't; we're just fooling ourselves.

We can fail to be open not only by deliberately hiding our thoughts and feelings, but also by merely avoiding uncomfortable subjects. A topic such as a former girlfriend or boyfriend, or an ex-spouse, can be avoided by simply hoping that it won't come up, and by assuming that until it does come up it isn't important. But the fact that you *hope* it won't come up indicates that it should be discussed. Any uncomfortable subject probably should come up at least once, so that it can be taken care of before it causes a problem.

Another obstacle to openness is a "peace at any price" attitude. This means going along with the situation simply to keep peace between the two of you. Maybe you just don't want to make a fuss about it. Or maybe it's too inconvenient to argue just then. Or perhaps the situation seems hopeless and nothing can be done about it so there's no point in confronting the issue.

One way to recognize a "peace at any price" attitude is when you find yourself saying, "We never argue or fight." If any of us can truthfully say that we never argue, there's probably something wrong somewhere. One or both may be ignoring or denying the realities that exist, or we may be covering up what we don't want to admit, or suppressing tension or frustration that will eventually explode.

It's so easy to fall into a "peace at any price" plight. Almost everyone does it sometime, even engaged couples. We did. Barb tells of a time during our dating days and our engagement:

> Bob was often late picking me up for our dates, and it began to bother me. I didn't say anything about it because most of the time it didn't really matter. And he *always* held in *his* anger, so.... But I was still angry inside that he wasn't at my door when he said he would be.

> I kept it hidden until one time when we were going to a wedding. He had gotten involved in some project and when he arrived he was quite late. He apologized, but that didn't really help. It had happened so often and this time it *was* important to me. I really blew up, far more explosively than the situation called for, and in fact I seriously reconsidered my decision to marry him. I wanted someone who thought I was important enough to him to keep his word.

> Fortunately, I realized, as I thought it through, that if I had complained earlier about his being late, it would have been much easier on both of us.

When we settle for "peace at any price" we're not really being truthful, and we hinder growth in our relationship. That kind of peace is false peace, and the price is too high to pay. We learned that!

We want a more intimate relationship than just living as room-mates, so we don't settle for less than complete honesty, or at least that's our goal. We want to overcome the fear and reluctance, so we make this decision to trust because we want our relationship to be as good as it *can* be.

The Other Side of Openness

Openness is not just one-sided, limited to revealing our inner selves. It also includes being open to listening to what our marriage partner is *saying,* or perhaps is *trying* to say. There may be times when he/she is baring his/her soul to you, and you feel uncomfortable hearing it. Perhaps he/she is chastising you for a behavior that you did or didn't do, and you don't want to hear it. Or he/she is asking for your help with something that means a lot to him/her and finds it difficult to express the need. Openness includes being willing to listen, and to help if necessary, so that he/she will trust enough to continue.

This side of openness can be just as difficult to engage in, but to avoid it is to deny our marriage partner the respect he/she deserves. Barb offers an example:

> I remember a time when Bob and I had had a strong disagree-ment about a political issue of importance to both of us. It wasn't something that we needed to agree on, but I wanted to discuss it before casting my ballot. Bob had already made up his mind, and wasn't really interested in what I had to say, but I wanted to consider his opinion in making my decision. Whenever I tried to talk about it, he would ignore me or change the subject. When he did that, I felt rejected. I had self-doubts. Why didn't he re-spect me enough to help me make this important decision? It set my "trust" level back a few notches.

Being open to what our partner wants to tell us, to listening with our mind and our heart, is perhaps as important a part of our relationship as being willing to reveal ourselves. And sometimes it takes more of a willingness to be trusted, to allow ourselves to be vulnerable to accept the confidence he/she places in us, than to trust.

As you've probably guessed, there are obstacles to this side of openness, too. And they're pretty much the same obstacles. And again, because we want more than just living as roommates, we shouldn't settle for less than complete openness, in both directions. We want to overcome the fear and reluctance, so we make the decision to trust and to *be* trusted because we want our relationship to be as good as it *can* be.

How Do We Overcome These Obstacles?

Most of the time we confront obstacles to openness by just gritting our teeth and doing it. We sit down together and calmly discuss the situation. And, lo and behold, it works! Other times, though, our discussion turns into an argument! But we've learned that arguing can be healthy and constructive when people love each other. If we argue fairly, it can be a positive way to communicate. It's another way of coming to understand each other, of bringing things into the open.

But beware! There are destructive ways to argue that can leave emotional scars. Verbal abuse is one thing to avoid; it isn't always *what* we say, but *how* we say it. If there's anger involved, it can turn to violence and, of course, physical violence of any level is **always** destructive; it indicates a psychological need and calls for professional help. We're talking here about arguing, or verbal fighting, not physical fighting.

We have a few guidelines for arguing, again inspired by ideas presented in Engaged Encounter. You'll find these helpful in making your arguments constructive (but we find them difficult to follow *all* the time).

GUIDELINES FOR ARGUING

1. No ugly name-calling or sarcasm. This only hurts feelings.
2. No third parties. It isn't fair to bring in friends or family or neighbors to take sides. The argument is between the two of you. If there is a need for a professional counselor, of course, get one; they normally don't take sides but help couples to see each other's point of view.
3. Stick to the subject. Especially when there is anger, it's easy to get off the track. Clarify the issue if necessary, so both understand what the argument is about. Bringing in other issues only confuses this situation. Deal with one at a time.
4. Argue about *current* topics. If something really bothers you, talk about it right away, before it grows out of proportion and the anger or resentment grows beyond reason. Also, if an issue has been settled in a previous argument, don't bring it up to re-hash as part of this one.
5. Don't use your partner's weaknesses as your ammunition. You know his or her vulnerabilities better than anyone, which buttons to push. To use that information in an argument can create a reluctance to be open in the future, and threaten to destroy the trust that has built up. You could win the argument, but lose respect.
6. Don't just clam up or storm off in anger if you feel you're "losing." Either finish the argument or agree to continue the discussion later, when both are rested and thinking more clearly. If the anger is so great that you feel you *must* leave, then do. But agree to resolve the issue as soon as possible. Recognize that the argument should have happened sooner.
7. Maintain a sense of humor. Don't be too rigid. Try to stay loose enough to laugh if something funny happens or the argument becomes ridiculous.

Friends of ours tell of an argument they had on the way home from the grocery store. The bickering continued as they were putting the groceries away and, for emphasis, she threw a head of lettuce on the floor with great force. As she says, "We had shredded lettuce the easy way, but it was a mess to clean up." In a situation like that, a good laugh may be just what's needed.

8. Listen. Repeat aloud the other's point of view to let him or her know that you've understood correctly. (Maybe you haven't.)

9. Talk about feelings and ideas in addition to the behavior involved. We're often more accepting of each other's actions when we understand the emotions on both sides.

10. Stay physically close to one another. An affectionate touch helps us to remember that we care about each other and that there is nothing that we cannot work out in love. Again, physical violence is *always* destructive and calls for professional help, so make sure the touch is gentle and affectionate!

Above all, remember that the *issue* is not the most important thing; **we** are. Being right is not as important as the quality of our relationship.

There are several positive aspects of arguing. For one thing, it can help us listen to each other in our feelings, needs, and hurts. Also, it helps us to reveal ourselves to each other as we express these feelings, needs, and hurts. It can also help us recognize our own irresponsibility or our responsibility in difficult situations, and can help us recognize our selfishness. It can help clear up misunderstandings. And it helps us discover where we really are with each other right at that moment – and can help get us back to where we want to be.

And, indeed, there are times when we shouldn't argue, such as when all we want to do is retaliate, cause pain, or make the other experience guilt. Those are childish things, but some adults still do them. We shouldn't argue when one or both of us is out of control. That's worth repeating – we shouldn't argue when one or both of us is out of control; better to call for "time out" and go back to it when all is calm again. And we shouldn't argue in public. If the issue is important, it will keep until there's privacy.

Remember that honesty and openness, total truthfulness, even when arguing, are foundations of a good relationship. Our arguing can build or destroy. The choice is ours, whether we want to grow or to hurt.

SUMMARY

To summarize all this, openness in communication is vital to any meaningful marriage. It's an absence of secrecy between the two, carried out in an atmosphere of love. There will often be a risk, and it might be uncomfortable at times, and there might be the temptation to settle for "peace at any price." We overcome the obstacles by depending on our desire for an intimate relationship. If our discussion becomes an argument, we turn to the guidelines for fair arguing.

Openness is a decision, like the decision to love. We're allowing ourselves to be vulnerable and we might be hurt. But we cannot grow closer without taking this risk. Honesty and openness provide the foundation of a good relationship.

There's a lot to reflect on this time. Again, write as much as you can, even if your fiancé already knows what you will say. Just because you've discussed it, that doesn't mean you've come to an agreement. Barb remembers asking one couple where they were going to be married and they said, simultaneously, "My church," then looked at each other in disbelief. They *had* discussed it, and had made a decision. But obviously one of them, perhaps both, didn't fully understand what that decision was!

Reflection #4

(20 minutes for writing, 15 minutes for discussion)

First, check off any area where you're not being totally open with your fiancé, areas in which you have difficulty revealing your thoughts, feelings, actions, etc.

☐ Fear of failure	☐ Responsibility of marriage
☐ Sex	☐ Children
☐ Religious faith	☐ Family relationships
☐ Job/career (yours/mine)	☐ Security
☐ Hobbies	☐ The way you treat me
☐ Personal habits	☐ Manners
☐ Drinking/drugs	☐ Dress
☐ Speech/grammar	☐ Educational goals
☐ Equality in marriage	☐ Friends
☐ Food	☐ Roles in marriage
☐ Finances	☐ Other (give details)

Write your thoughts and feelings, negative as well as positive, on each of those checked. (Hint: those that make you uncomfortable are the ones you need to open up on most.)

- The area I want to know more about *you* is…
- An unusual habit I have that I have not told you about is…

- One way I've changed since we became engaged is…
- One way *you've* changed since we became engaged is…
- A time when I was hurt by your bluntness was…
- A secret I've kept because I was afraid of losing you is…
- The parts of my inner self that I prefer to keep private include…
- I'd like to know more about your ex-fiancé/ex-spouse in the area of…
- Regarding my ex-fiancé/ex-spouse, I want to tell you more about…
- "Peace at any price" reminds me of the time I…
- A time I disagreed with you and didn't say anything was…
- I don't always let you know when I disagree with you because…
- We could improve our arguing by…
- The hardest guideline for me to follow when arguing is…
- A time I felt we shouldn't have argued was…

5

You Expected <u>What</u>?!

Acknowledging Differences

This is another topic that couples tell us is very helpful, so do read carefully and make notes in the margins. We may only mention briefly something that is very important to you and you might want to refer to it later.

A good marriage is not just living together, but it's a continually deepening relationship due, partly, to the openness we've talked about and the honesty that goes along with it. In the last section we gave you a chance to open up on some new topics. Realize that the openness we're talking about is not a one-day exercise, but in a good marriage it becomes a way of life. If we don't continually strive to be open, we can actually become "closed" to one another, and our relationship suffers. This openness includes acknowledging our differences, no matter how large or small they seem to be. The fact is, a marriage is more likely to run smoothly if we acknowledge our differences. One reason our communication might become closed is those differences.

We're All Different

We can almost hear you thinking, "What differences? What are you talking about?" But they're there. Even couples who've known

Prepare for Your Marriage

each other for years have differences – many kinds, for many reasons. First of all, there are the various ideas and expectations that we each bring into marriage. This isn't bad; it's just the way people are. Then there are the differences we know are there – they're obvious – but we choose to deny or ignore them. And sometimes a difference comes when a change occurs in one person after the marriage begins, and the other can't or won't accept it.

When our differences cause conflicts, we might avoid discussing the difference, and can become closed to each other in that area. When the topic comes up, we clam up. It's important that we learn to acknowledge, respect, and appreciate our marriage partner's individuality, even if it's different from what we expected or want it to be. Let's look at various kinds of differences more closely.

Differences Before Marriage

First let's consider the differences that are there before the marriage begins, differences that most couples have. Virtually everyone has had preconceived ideas on what married life will be like. Maybe like single life, or like their parent's marriage, or friends' marriages, or maybe their own previous marriage. And we each probably assume that our fiancé shares the same expectations. But what happens when her concept is different from his? Since she grew up with *her* parents' marriage, and he grew up in *his*, they're bound to have a different picture of what marriage is like. That was true for us too, of course, but we can't remember that we ever actually talked about this. More likely, we each assumed that his/her thoughts were exactly the same – after all, we'd been dating for three years and were engaged for half that time! But it's not very wise to make assumptions like that. For just one example, Barb tells us:

> My family always ate a light, early evening meal, and that's what
> I expected would happen in my marriage. But Bob's family had
> meat, vegetables, potatoes, salad, and dessert every evening at
> 6 p.m. You can guess what *he* expected.

Sometimes we realize the difference is there but we choose to ignore or deny it. We might either ignore or deny that they even exist or we deny that they might affect our marriage. Barb continues:

> We're guilty here, too. We knew the difference about the evening meal was there, but we both just ignored it. We denied that it would affect our marriage. After all, how important can a meal be, right? Wrong! We finally had to sit down and talk about it anyway. It would have been easier on us if we'd talked about it right off, instead of assuming.

Another reason we might ignore a difference that we already know about is because we think we can change our partner. But hear this loud and clear: you cannot change anyone!!! People change only when and if they *want* to. It is *their* decision. A change in behavior requires a change in attitude; a person must become convinced that a change will benefit him or her. She might change her behavior because that's what he wants, but it isn't *his* choice to make for her. And conversely, she can't change him. Only *he* can change himself, when and if he chooses to.

As Bob relates:

> In my earlier years I wasn't what you'd call a natty dresser – I'd reach for a pair of pants, a shirt, and socks and get dressed. If the combination looked like an old crayon box, I didn't notice. But Barb did. After our wedding, she decided that I should have a "coordinated look." She would carefully hang a green print shirt with green pants, a brown tweed jacket with brown pants, and so on. Then she'd lecture me when I wore the green shirt with the brown jacket and burgundy pants! I thought it looked okay. The point is, she just couldn't change me!

> But I could change myself! And I did. Well, I try harder now. Our love for each other is what made me want to change. She stopped lecturing me and accepted me as I am because she loves me (although she does still occasionally snicker as I'm

selecting my wardrobe for the day). And I try to please her because I love her.

We might also ignore some differences we already know about because we expect that *marriage* will magically change our partner. For example, the new wife of a once-a-week golfer might expect him to give up his weekly game because "after all, he's married now." That *might* happen, but if it doesn't, and a conflict arises because her expectation wasn't met, there's a good chance of becoming closed to each other in this area, with one of us clamming up and refusing to talk about it. Drinking and drugs and the amount of time spent with friends, either individually or as a couple, are other areas where people commonly expect magical changes. There are many other situations. You can probably think of some that are in your life right now.

As a further illustration of what this kind of thinking can lead to, let's say we have a wife who loves to shop and enjoy the nice things money can buy. The husband feels more secure with a comfortable savings account or investments. She denies that the difference will affect the marriage, thinking, "No problem – I spend, he saves; we balance each other!" But maybe at the same time he's thinking, "I'll teach her how to save, show her the value of this kind of security and she'll change her attitude." Can you see the clash they're headed for? Or maybe she's thinking, "He'll change after we're married and we have two incomes," at the same time he's thinking, "She'll change after we're married – she'll feel secure and outgrow her spending binges." There's certainly disillusionment in their future. Any of those things might happen, and they might *all* happen! You can see that this kind of situation can easily lead to conflict if it isn't faced early, and preferably before the wedding.

Change After the Marriage Begins

Changes after the wedding can also create differences that we might want to ignore or deny. Sometimes after a couple has been married a while one partner will undergo a change in ideas or beliefs or habits or whatever, and the other can have trouble accepting that change. For example, one person may learn a new hobby, maybe sailing, and begin to spend more and more time on the water. But the other isn't interested in sailing and gets left at home every weekend. They don't talk about it, though; they might even try to pretend there's no problem. When they do talk about it, they argue. So they avoid the topic, and they become closed to each other in that area. Not good! It's especially not good if an increasing amount of time is spent on sailing, and the two are separated more and more. How can they develop a deeper, closer relationship when they don't spend time together?

The fact is, we do continually change as individuals, learning and discovering new interests. So we can expect new differences between us at any time. That's why continual openness is important throughout marriage, not just in the beginning. Acceptance of each other, in spite of changes or lack of changes, is also important.

More Obstacles

Obstacles to acknowledging our differences are similar to the obstacles to openness. There's fear, this time a fear of being different. Our tendency is to deny or hide our personal differences, because we're afraid of being *too* different. It's hard to admit to something that might cause problems between us. Barb was guilty of this:

> When we were dating, I pretended to like classical music because I thought that was what Bob wanted in a wife and if I didn't like it he might look for someone who did, and I might lose him. And I often ignored or hid my anger because he was so easy-going I was sure he wouldn't like anger in anyone else. I was afraid he'd see us as incompatible.

> It didn't occur to me that I couldn't pretend forever! And I learned that those differences don't magically go away. I still get angry, though I show it more than I did then, and Bob still likes classical

music more than I do. Those differences are still there, years later.

We might ignore differences because we think that they take away from our oneness, but they don't have to. In fact, differences can add dimension to our relationship. Here's a good example from Barb:

> I like to play tennis and I used to play a lot (although I haven't played much recently). Bob plays, but he has never liked it as much as I. My activity led us both to some interesting experiences such as learning how to run tournaments, even winning a few trophies, traveling to other areas to play or to watch major tennis stars. It even led us to a few very nice vacation spots. And of course we made many, many friends through the social activities connected with tennis. Since the interest in tennis was mostly mine, I doubt that Bob would have had those experiences or made those friendships – and they've been good ones!

We sometimes ignore or deny differences because it becomes more convenient and more comfortable not to talk about them. Maybe it's easier for us to each keep our separate interests than to face our differences. To illustrate this, Barb says:

> I could have kept my tennis activities to myself, never inviting him to come along and be a part of the fun, and let him do whatever he wanted to do.

Or maybe one sees or suspects there' a difference but doesn't want to give up or give in to the other. Again, from Barb:

> I might have been afraid that Bob would not want me to go off to the tournaments and luncheons or even the regular playing, and I surely wouldn't have wanted to give it up just because he doesn't like it – I enjoy those things!

What to Do About Our Differences

The problem is not necessarily the differences themselves. The problem may be that we think the differences don't matter – we *assume* they will not develop into a problem. The fact is that differences cannot always be resolved and, if not, this should be realized and faced now so that it can be accepted or somehow handled before the marriage begins.

An example of a serious problem is when one of the partners wants to have children right away and the other doesn't ever want children at all. A problem like that *must* be settled before the marriage begins, or it will surely be a short-lived marriage, if there's a marriage at all. Another example happened to friends of ours. He was an older fellow, retired, with a "comfortable" income, looking for someone to share his golden years. She was maybe 15 years younger, a working woman, looking for companionship and security. They seemed very happy during their courtship. After the wedding they discovered that her sexual appetite was far greater than his; he *couldn't* change and she *wouldn't* accept his limitations. Their marriage lasted three very unhappy months. They both would have been spared the unhappiness if only they'd had the courage to discuss their expectations.

But just acknowledging differences, admitting that they exist, isn't enough. They must be dealt with, in whatever way is necessary to make your two lives compatible. Over the years we've learned that some of our differences are good and can complement each other. She likes to cook, he likes to eat! Others may simply need to be accepted. Bob says:

> I've accepted that Barb enjoys tennis; she has accepted that I enjoy classical music. No substantial changes were required here.

Some differences will be compromised. Again Bob give us an example:

I like my music loud, Barb doesn't, so I wear earphones; Barb continued to play tennis, but only when it didn't interfere with our mutual activities.

Perhaps some differences will even need to be minimized by a behavior change, such as the husband who rarely goes camping anymore because the wife doesn't enjoy camping. (Again, in this case, it must be *his* decision to change; any pressure on him will surely cause resentment.)

Note that we're not saying that if one plays golf they both should or that one should quit. And no "If you love me, you'll change." In a long-lasting marriage, we learn to accept each other as we are; that's part of our commitment to each other. But realize that some differences are very difficult to resolve, and it's best to learn what has to be accepted before the commitment is made. The knowing what our differences are is where a more profound love for the *real* person can grow and develop.

But...

Couples sometimes think a difference has been accepted or re-solved, then later find that each thought the other had agreed to his or her way – and find that the difference was as great, maybe even greater, than before. This is why we ask you to write on all the items at the end of each section, even though you think your fiancé already knows what you'll say. When you read what your fiancé has actually put down in writing, you might be surprised.

Common areas where this sort of thing can occur are careers and ambitions. Maybe your goal is set too high or too low for your fiancé. Or maybe your idea of success is not the same as his/hers. Or your value of the importance of success may be greater than his/hers, or less.

Another area is postponing and planning a family. Maybe you have fears about being a parent. Maybe you want to remain child-less, or you think he or she does. Maybe there are pressures from friends or family for you to start a family right after the wedding. These things may have been talked about but not really settled yet. If not, you really can't be sure that your differences are compatible.

Biggies

There are a few topics where differences can cause problems for even the strongest, best-intentioned relationships. Again, these issues should be discussed, and settled if possible, before the marriage begins.

Biggie No. 1: Religion

This is just one area where we may not want to face our differences, particularly our religious beliefs and practices. This issue isn't just for those of us who are practicing our beliefs; it's also for those who might *want* to but haven't. The differences may be very obvious, but we may avoid the topic because it seems impossible to resolve. For example, a combination of Jewish and Christian or Catholic and Protestant can be a major problem for some couples. Our differences weren't that great but there were some. As Barb tells it:

> We both grew up as Lutherans, so we had a common base. But Bob's dad was active in their church, mine wasn't. Not a big thing, but it could have caused disagreements, such as would I want my husband to go off to meetings? Would I go with him? I knew I wouldn't want to join the women's groups – would he want me to?

There are questions in the area of religion that we didn't have to confront, but many couples do. For example if we're of different faiths, whose church should we join? Should we try to find a church we both like that is something different from either of our present churches? Can one of us convert to the faith of the other? If one of us has no faith or if we are of different faiths and neither converts, will we continue to practice our religion? In whose faith will our children be raised? Whose responsibility will their spiritual up-bringing be? If neither of us is involved with a church now, will we look into it? Will we wait until after we have children to get involved in a church? These are questions that might apply to you. Whether you are religiously active or not they should be fully explored and the options should be agreed upon before the marriage begins.

Family Values

This is yet another important area where we may choose to ignore or overlook differences, our family's values. Whether we realize it or not (and whether we *like* it or not!), we all bring some of our family's personality traits into our marriage. And the differences there can create problems, too. Barb tells us:

> One difference we had before we married was that Bob's family seemed to be a little more demonstrative than mine, especially the older women. My family was big on family gatherings, but we didn't hug everyone that came through the door, as Bob's grandmother and his aunts seemed to. I didn't feel uncomfortable, but it bothered me that I hugged *his* aunt, but didn't hug my own!

> (That was almost 40 years ago; times have changed, and so have I – now I hug my aunts, my brothers, my friends, my pastor!)

A second example, from Bob:

> Before we were married, one area where I saw a significant difference in our families was in the attitude toward higher education. It was clear that both families managed to support themselves, but my family considered college a natural continuation after high school. Barb's family left it for each to decide when the time came. By the time we married, I had grown to accept and love her family despite this difference. No one had to change to make it work, but we did have to *accept* one another.

Differences in families may seem unimportant to you right now, things that will easily be remedied after the wedding. But it isn't always so easy. We each had to ask ourselves, "Do I really accept him/her and this family? Am I sure they truly accept me? Or do I expect them to change for me?" Family values can be especially important if we live close to other family members.

Rich and Not-So-Rich

Another important difference might be in the financial backgrounds. One may be from a wealthy family and so accustomed to the finer things that money can bring that he or she is unaware that these are luxuries. And the other isn't. Questions to consider: Which lifestyle will the couple choose? How will the other adjust? How will their families accept this choice? Will either family help financially? How will the other family accept that? How would *you* accept it?

An engaged couple we met a while back fit that very pattern. She was from a wealthy family and didn't want to give up all the luxuries that her father's money could buy for them. He was not wealthy and wanted to support her himself in the best way that he could, which was far below what she was accustomed to. Fortunately, they realized that this was a difference that was already causing a problem, one that would have to be resolved if their marriage was going to last beyond the Hawaiian honeymoon that Daddy was paying for! Differences in financial backgrounds can cause <u>BIG</u> problems which are best worked out before the marriage begins.

SUMMARY

We've covered a lot of information in this section, so let's recap here:

- In a good, lasting marriage openness extends to not only recognizing but openly admitting, and sometimes rejoicing in, our differences.
- Every married couple has differences. When they might cause conflict, we tend to ignore or deny them. It's important to openly identify them and admit to them.

- Some differences are known before the marriage begins, but we ignore or deny them; we often expect them to magically disappear after the wedding, or we tell ourselves that it doesn't matter.
- Some differences are due to changes that occur after the marriage is underway; continuing to discuss differences is an indication of open communication.
- There are several obstacles to acknowledging our differences, including various fears, unwillingness to give in or give up, or "peace at any price."
- We need to admit to our differences and deal with them by either accepting, compromising, appreciating, or maybe even changing our own habits.
- We shouldn't ignore differences because the fact is that some cannot be resolved, or accepted (Big trouble!).

It's *okay* to be different and to disagree, but know what those differences are and what you are disagreeing about! Small differences can grow into big problems. As Barb realized:

> Bob could have developed some other interest while I was busy playing tennis, some activity I might not want him to do, or he might have resented my being away and developed an anger that eventually would explode.

It's much easier to talk about differences in the beginning, and it's easier to resolve them when they're small or newly discovered. It's important that we learn to acknowledge, respect, accept, and appreciate our partner's individuality, even if it's different from what we expected. This can and often does turn out to be an enriching factor.

Again, there is a lot to reflect on. Still, write as much as you can on each one. This is such an important area it's worth going back to at a later time as well.

Reflection #5

(Minimum writing time 20 minutes; discussion 15 minutes)

First, check off the areas where you believe you have differences:

☐ Ideas about duties of husband and wife

☐ Interests in outdoor or in-door activities

☐ Personality opposites

☐ Time with friends

☐ Family involvement

☐ Family values

☐ Money: one is a spender, the other a saver

☐ Family cultural back-ground

☐ Financial background

☐ Religious faith

☐ Other _____

Put an X at those you've talked about; explain those not talked about.

- The differences I've ignored because I think you will change are…
- Difference I expected to disappear simply because we're married are…
- The differences I see a need for compromise are…
- Differences where I'm willing to make a change are…
- The differences I acknowledge and accept are…
- The differences I am still hesitant to talk to you about are…
- Differences that still need to be resolved are…
- One of the ways I'm like my father or mother is…

- One of the ways you're like your father or mother is…
- One thing about you that I have thought marriage might change is…
- One doubt I've had about getting married is…
- One doubt I've had about marrying *you* is…
- Expectations that I have about our marriage include…
- Activities that I expect to quit, continue alone, or invite you are…
- Activities that I expect you'll quit, continue alone, or invite me are…
- I want us to (attend/not attend) church together because…
- I want us to join (my/your/a new church) because…
- If you choose to not attend church I will go alone because…
- I want our children raised in (my/your) faith because…

6

Okay, Here's the Deal
What Kind of Marriage Will <u>We</u> Have?

This section is one of our favorites. It doesn't fit the pattern of previous sections; this one doesn't lead to problem solving, but it makes us feel good! In this section we'll point out the difference between a secular marriage and a Christian marriage, from our viewpoint, and we'll help you learn how to achieve fulfillment in *your* marriage, using these principles. If you or your fiancé are not Christians, please continue reading anyway. You'll probably pick up some helpful tips on making your marriage better.

A Secular vs. A Christian Marriage

For some people, making their marriage legal is all they really want. To do that in California requires only four things: a marriage license from the county clerk, meet state and county requirements (blood test, minimum age), some sort of ceremony before a qualified representative of the state, and the certificate from that official, properly recorded. This kind of marriage seems hardly more than a convenient arrangement, to abandon when it no longer suits the purpose or when the going gets rough. Sometimes it even includes a written contract with conditions by which the two parties must live, or conditions they agree to in case of divorce. Even before they marry, they're preparing to divorce!

But in a Christian marriage, one that follows God's plan for marriage, the union is far more than a legal agreement, even a legal agreement that's life-long. God's plan for marriage *includes* the legal agreement but it also includes a total commitment, made on faith and trust in each other and in God, not really knowing where it will lead. Remember how we talked earlier about changes that might occur in one of you? And how sometimes it might be difficult for the other to accept those changes? That possibility is made clear in the traditional Christian marriage vow when we say, "for better or for worse." In God's plan marriage expresses a unique love between a man and a woman. In John 15:12 Jesus commands us to

"Love one another as I have loved you."

This commandment was the inspiration for the traditional marriage vow. (It was directed toward *all* of His followers, of course, but it becomes even more relevant when two people of the opposite sex plan to live together for the rest of their lives.) Marriage is our opportunity to love each other unconditionally, as He loves us, to be to each other as He is to us. A result of this kind of love between a husband and wife is that each of us can become more complete. We not only develop our own potential more fully, but we benefit by being part of another's life. As Bob has experienced:

> Because of Barb's support and her faith in my competence, I earned a higher degree of education than I would have on my own. And I seriously doubt that I would be helping you prepare for your marriage right now if it wasn't for Barb's superior ability to organize and her strong interest in making other marriages better. That's just one way that I've benefited from being a part of her life.

Love and Marriage, In God's Plan

Like most of you, the two of us began our relationship as acquaintances, then we became friends, and before long we realized that we were "in love" with one another. In God's plan for marriage, He calls us to live that love in our daily lives, deepening our friendship. We do that by continually focusing on and ministering to one another, each helping and serving and supporting the other in whatever ways we can, just as we did when we first realized that we were in love many years ago.

For example, we listen, truly listen, to each other, going beyond the words and trying to understand the deeper feelings that are there. We take interest in and make an effort to accept every aspect of the other's life. The *good* is easy to accept, of course, and we make the effort to accept the not-so-good. We also continually try to be open with each other, letting the other know our true thoughts, feelings, dreams, and sharing those things that we usually don't want to share with anyone else. We offer support by affirming each other, by being aware of what a treasure we are to each other, and letting the other know how we feel about that. Barb says:

> I help and support Bob by letting him know how much I appreciate his intelligence, his dependability, and all his other blessings. And by getting my focus back to him when I've let it drift to something else.

We also minister by healing each other. When one of us is hurt or troubled, the other is a source of comfort and strength. This ministering to each other, helping and supporting, is how we live our love for each other. Maybe you've never thought of yourself as a minister, but you *can* be.

Remember that Jesus said, "Love one another as I have loved you." He wants us to live in unconditional love, to love each other the way He loves us. That means we are to love without keeping score, without "doing my share" then waiting for the other to do his/hers. In

God's plan for marriage, it's not a 50-50 proposition; it's a 100-100 proposition, an unconditional promise of love under any circumstances. That's how He loves us. He wants us each to give 100%, even when the other gives nothing, and to be willing to take 100%, even when we can give nothing. Barb remembers:

> During my childhood I had heard that marriage was a 50-50 deal, but I knew that there were times when either Mom or Dad seemed to be giving more than half. I knew they did it willingly, but I didn't know that that was God's plan, and I'm pretty sure *they* didn't either – it was just the natural, loving thing to do.
>
> Now that I'm in a marriage of my own, when either of us falls short, I focus on our marriage relationship with 100% of my effort, even when it is rough. My commitment to Bob, and knowing that he is committed to me, helps get us through those rough spots.

His Special Gift for Us

God's plan for marriage offers us the opportunity for a relationship more intimate than any other, because He asks for a total commitment to each other. And He asks that we continue to show love for each other daily. We've found that these two things, the commitment followed by daily showing our love for each other, cause what started out as an acquaintanceship to develop into a deep intimacy, one that can be matched by no other relationship. We call this "unity."

Unity, as we use the term, is "a state of being one, whole, or complete in a marriage relationship." It's the result of a friendship so deep and so intimate that the two people can feel as one. It's a measure of the quality of our marriage. This unity is something intangible and somewhat mystical. We're aware of it through that sense of belonging together, the identity we share as husband and wife. Our Number 1 priority, after God, is that our marriage relationship is the most important thing in our lives, no matter what. Not jobs, not vacations, not hobbies, not money, but US!

Most of us have grown up in a world that tells us that our goal in life should be happiness and that a good marriage means happiness, constant bliss, having lots of expensive things, and so on. From early on, we get the message that happiness is achieved through possessions and status. And sometimes it works – or it seems to. But even in those early years we learned that this kind of happiness doesn't last; it wears off with time. You can probably think of several examples of this in your own experiences. Remember your first bicycle? Or your first car? Remember how happy you were? But does that bike or that car still bring you happiness? Probably not. Only the memories remain. Or maybe something you got five years ago or five months ago or even last month. Right now it probably isn't giving you happiness. How about your engagement ring? The ring itself you're probably used to by now. The happiness you feel comes from what the ring *symbolizes*, not from the ring itself. Wouldn't you be just as happy without the ring? The point we're trying to make here is that we can't find true, lasting happiness through possessions.

Happiness, bliss, and success come and go throughout life. Even though we may be happy today, something could happen tomorrow to change that, such as getting a serious illness, or going out to the parking lot and finding your car smashed, or losing your job because the company is closing. We have no control over the many outside forces that can temporarily destroy our happiness. Does the lack of feeling happy mean the marriage is a bad one? No, it doesn't. Therefore, happiness and constant bliss, by themselves, can't really be the sign of a *good* marriage. Likewise, their absence doesn't necessarily mean it's a bad marriage, does it?

God's plan is that our ultimate goal in marriage should be unity. His plan for us includes the development of our friendship into an intimacy and caring so deep that nothing short of death can destroy it.

True love will be there because possessions and external circumstances won't dominate our lives; our love for each other will dominate. But realize that unity doesn't automatically develop in every marriage. We have to do our part. It takes a special effort and desire. Even when we're angry with one another or disappointed, we can remember that these are temporary feelings, no matter how intense. But our commitment to each other's well-being is permanent.

For us, as Christians, we believe that our love for each other is an extension of God's love for us and, like His love, our love can exist in spite of outside influences and fluctuations. Our unity has developed from an open and trusting relationship, characterized by our love for one another in all circumstances. At first it's hard to trust each other and to believe in each other that much, to allow ourselves to be that vulnerable. It takes a while to be comfortable with it. But without that openness and the trust, the intimacy would never develop; it would never exist. The decision to love each other in all circumstances would be much harder to make.

Living our marriage as God has planned, developing our unity, means that we share each other's good times and bad times – our joys are doubled, our sorrows are divided by two. Barb gives a few examples:

> When Bob gets a promotion, we both rejoice; when I do an exceptional job on a project, he's as proud as I am. And when my father suffered through a long illness before his death, when my brother was seriously injured in an auto accident, Bob was by my side giving me the support I needed. When Bob's mother died unexpectedly, I put all my activities on hold so we could travel together to be with his family at the funeral. It's nice to have intimate companionship.

Contrary to what you might have thought, unity does not come from the two of us trying to copy each other, or be the same kind of persons, each giving up things we like because the other doesn't like it. It doesn't come from always being together, or from one of us always submitting to the other's demands or desires. Unity doesn't develop from any of those things. Again, it develops over an extended period of mutual openness and growing trust and trustworthiness between us. And it involves repeatedly making the decision to love.

Even with our unity, the two of us are individuals and we always will be. We will always have some differences and perhaps one or more can't ever be reconciled. We simply agree to disagree, while respecting each other for the good person that is there. In our individuality we are still one as a couple, and we live, love, argue, and work together because we are committed to each other. Our happiness isn't based on possessions or events. **Our *unity* has become the basis of our happiness**.

The unity created by our love can and should be a source of strength when things go wrong. One of the best things about our marriage is its ability to offer protection and security against the outside world. During rough times we can turn to each other and face the problems *together*, confident in our love and our oneness as a couple.

Our Marriage Has a Purpose

Your marriage can become a part of God's plan, just as ours is. We chose to live according to His plan because He has a *purpose* for our marriage, and for yours if you choose, and that purpose is to spread love to others. The two of us are a sign, a testimony to others that God's love is real. Our love for each other is perhaps the best reflection of God's love. It can be seen through our behavior in our togetherness, our fidelity, our healing of each other, and our forgiveness. In 1 John 4:8 we learn that "God is love." We are a mirror of His love and forgiveness when we reflect His love to those around us. And as a couple, we're like the disciples who were sent by Jesus into the world two by two. Luke 10:1 says, "…the Lord…sent them on ahead of Him, two by two, into every town and place where He

Himself was about to come." God calls us to go into the world and show His love by reflecting that love to everyone we meet. Remember these words of some wise sage, "Love wasn't put in your heart to stay; love isn't love 'til you give it away."

So how do we do that? It isn't hard. We can easily reflect God's love to each of our families, such as when we took the time to send Bob's brother a birthday card, or when Barb phones or e-mails our daughters, just to make contact, or sends her Mom a note to cheer her up or let her know we're thinking about her. Other examples are when we offered to help her sister move, when we sent a letter to congratulate our niece and nephew on their new baby or sent Bob's aunt a newspaper article we were sure she'd be interested in, when we offer to baby-sit with our own grandchildren so their parents can have some time for each other, or send get-well wishes to a new friend. In short, whenever we take the time to be a loving sister and brother, aunt and uncle, parent, grandparent, friend, acquaintance, or whatever. It's easy and it makes us feel good. When you think about it, if *we* don't show them love, who will?

Memorable Times Become Traditions

In our own little family we have the greatest opportunities for the expression of love. Often these opportunities develop into traditions, making everyday occasions special and special occasions memorable. We're talking now of those events that are anticipated as a time of love and fellowship between family members. Barb remembers:

> When I was young, the whole family was always involved in any graduation, or performance in a play or recital, or a Boy Scout ceremony – anything that was special for one was special for all of us. At the time we thought, "That's just what you do." But as I look back I can see that these occasions brought our family closer together and built some pretty good memories for all of us, memories that each of us treasure today.

Some of these traditions we carried into our own marriage. I remember how eager I was to make costumes for our children's Halloween fun, as my mom had done for me. Many experiences don't start out as traditions but they end up giving us all some very warm, loving feelings as we reminisce – bedtime stories and prayers, meal-time conversations, our summers at the cabin, and so on. The loving feelings create the reason for them to become traditions.

Adopting some of Bob's family's traditions helped me to become an accepted member of *his* family. I remember how pleased his mother was when she visited us at Christmas and saw that I had baked all *their* favorite holiday cookies as a part of *our* celebration, too."

We've discovered through times like those that without togetherness there *is* no family. Showing love for each other through our traditions has a way of bringing added stability to our family. Our traditions are a source of heart-warming, lasting memories. They give each member of the family a sense of identity, of belonging, of being part of our unit.

Love Thy Neighbor

Of course it's easy to show love for our friends and neighbors, too, by inviting them out for dinner or to our home for a visit, letting them know we respect their opinion by asking for advice, letting them know when we need help, nominating them for an award, or just taking the time to celebrate their special occasions or to share their grief.

As a couple, we can start showing love for others as our marriage begins. One way to show love for friends and relatives, of course, is to invite them to your wedding. If you can, include those who've been an important influence in your life, even though they might not know it, such as a favorite teacher, or the parents of a friend.

We attended a garden wedding a while back where the entire families of both the bride and the groom were given corsages or boutonnieres and then, just before the ceremony began, each person wearing a flower was introduced to everyone. It took only a moment, but you can be sure that each of them felt very special and important. At a recent reception each table held a camera so that the guests could take pictures of everyone at their table. The bride and groom wanted to *see* us all having a good time, making sure that every guest was included in their photo album. Then, along with a thank-you note, we found a copy of the photo of us.

These are just a few of the ways to let people know from the beginning of your marriage that they mean something in your lives. Begin thinking of others, because you'll need enough ideas to last a lifetime!

SUMMARY

To summarize all of this, realize that, whether you're believers or not, God does have a plan for marriage, a plan which makes it much more than just a legal contract. His plan calls for a total commitment, a daily decision to love each other. When we choose to follow His plan, we continue to treat each other with the same love and caring that we knew during our engagement, but now each being willing to give 100% of our effort to the other, asking nothing in return – that's unconditional love. This kind of marriage is a gift from God, a deeper and more intimate relationship than any other.

In God's plan each married couple is a demonstration to others that His love is real; we are to spread His love to everyone we meet. His plan and His purpose for our marriage is really a lifestyle which He offers us, a way of living together that can provide a rich and very fulfilling life. As Barb says:

> I've found that the more I give to Bob, the more I feel the depth of his love and the more I realize fulfillment in my own life.

We can both say the same about others: the more we give to others, the more we feel the depth of God's love and the more we realize fulfillment in our life as a couple. So you see, every man and woman in marriage has a choice:

    a. To live a life of self-concern, limited only to self-fulfillment.
    b. To develop a deep, tender, responsible relationship with your beloved and with others in the world around you.

Which do you think is God's plan for the two of *you*? Which do you think will lead to a long-lasting and fulfilling marriage?

On to the Reflection

Reflection #6

(Minimum writing time is 15 minutes; discussion 15 minutes)

- I prefer a (total commitment / legal agreement) because…
- I can show love for you every day for the rest of our lives by…
- Committing myself to you 100%, maybe getting 0% in return, is…
- A time when I tried to find happiness through possessions was…
- A time when an external circumstance destroyed our happiness was…
- I (do/don't) trust you enough to develop unity because…
- We could achieve unity in our marriage if we…
- Being chosen by you, above all others, means…
- A special quality we as a couple have to share with others is…
- Specific ways we can share love with our families/friends include…
- Traditions of my family that I want to continue in our marriage include…
- Traditions of *your* family that I want to continue in our marriage include..

7

Decisions, Decisions, Decisions!
Making Important Decisions in Marriage

This section, as you can guess, goes back to the problem-solving pattern. It's an important topic, and it's a long one, so be prepared to dig deep.

Decision #1: To Be Life-Giving

First, you're probably wondering what "life-giving" means, so let's define it. It means to be nourishing, encouraging, supportive, and up-lifting to others. When one of us praises the other, let's say on work he or she has done, it's life-giving, especially if the praise is given when other people can hear.

The opposite of this is to be threatening, down-grading, or verbally abusive. If either of us insults or belittles the other for any reason, that is *not* being life-giving. That's being destructive. It's particularly harmful when done in front of others.

To be life-giving is more than non-harmful, though. It's more than not infringing on another's rights and not hurting him/her. To be life-giving is to *advance* life in some way, bringing more life to another person, drawing out the full potential of another person, showing that person that he/she is always lovable. Of course, in marriage that other person is our spouse.

For us, loving each other includes a decision to behave in a life-giving, nurturing manner. The ideas of openness, listening, and trusting one another with our inner selves are central to the concept of a life-giving, unselfish philosophy. When we're open and reveal our deepest thoughts and feelings to each other, we tend to be more sensitive, attentive, concerned, and patient with one another. It's life-giving and supportive to show concern when one senses that the other is upset about something. We can bring forth the inherent goodness of each other by reflecting back the goodness we see. In Bob's words:

> It's life-giving and boosts Barb's happiness when I compliment her on a project that she's working on, or when I tell her how delighted our daughter was when Barb sent flowers for her birthday. I'm also life-giving when I let Barb nourish me when I'm down, such as when she sympathized at the death of my grandmother, or when she listened lovingly as I told her how discouraged I was about a project I was working on.

That kind of approach allows the possibility of the rich, full, and abundant life that Jesus talked about. Now, how do we apply this concept to our decisions?

Making Decisions in a Life-Giving Manner

Almost everything we do in life is the result of a decision we've made. We make decisions every day. And one of the more difficult things to adjust to in marriage is making *mutual* decisions, particularly if either person has been a single adult for any length of time. Most people just get used to making decisions on their own and when they suddenly have to consider another person, it can be difficult. But in marriage it's necessary.

In addition to considering another person's opinion and feelings, we're expected to be life-giving and unselfish in those decisions, *and* to meet our responsibilities! That can really be hard sometimes! It helps, though, to ask yourself, "Does this decision, or this behavior, bring life and encouragement? Does it strengthen the important relationships in my life?" And, for Christians and other believers, the most important question, "Is this what *God* would choose for me to do?"

We have four guidelines that we use to help us in making major decisions in a life-giving manner that we'd like to pass along to you.

1. Prayer. Be aware of God's closeness to you. Ask His guidance. Barb read recently that the answers to our problems are already within us; all we need to do is find them. Prayer helps us find the answers.

2. Get all the facts you can.

    a. Clarify your purpose and what needs to be decided.

    b. Set the criteria: What do you want to achieve? Make it specific.

    c. Establish priorities among the criteria. Rate them 1-10.

    d. List various solutions to meeting the criteria. Rate them 1-10.

    e. Multiply the rating of each criterion by the rating of each solution.

    f. Add up the scores of each solution. The best solution, then, is obvious.

    g. Cross-check: What could go wrong? What could you do about it?

    h. Consult authorities you trust; consider each other's opinion.

    i. Ask yourself, "Is this solution life-giving?"

3. Discuss it , then make the decision together, with a life-giving attitude.

4. Evaluate, and later re-evaluate, the decision as needs, wants, and circumstances change.

These guidelines can apply for most major decisions in life, but some can be made with less detail. For our purposes here, we'll focus on decisions regarding the relationships in marriage.

Making Decisions in Marriage

Our first priority in decision-making is to be life-giving toward each other. We need to continually make decisions in the area of our relationship because we discover new things about each other as we grow and change in our behavior and in our attitudes as we mature. As Bob says:

> I'm more active in our church and in other volunteer work than I was 20 years ago. That often means evening meetings. When I tutor my ESL/literacy student, it requires preparation time. Barb is life-giving and understanding when she lets me go without complaining about being left alone so often.

To be life-giving is to help each other grow, and not trap our partner in a role or pattern. Our love is not conditional upon always staying exactly the same. Bob continues:

> A while back Barb learned to do landscape design. I was life-giving and supportive of her talent when I agreed that we should start our own design business. More recently, she's been conducting communication workshops and is halfway through writing a book on oral presentation skills; I've agreed to be her assistant and do the accounting for her. My life-giving attitude has encouraged her to apply her skills in new ways.

> We need to keep our decisions mutual, not one-sided. The *ideas* of going into business, offering workshops, and authoring a book were hers, but the decisions about the projects were mutual.

Decisions about Money: Earning, Spending, Saving

We need to make decisions about the money we earn, too. Handling money is a topic in itself but there are some questions to keep in mind where decisions will be needed. Will both earn? (This is really a decision between time and money and we'll get into that later.) If both earn, will we live on one income and save the other, or will we live on both incomes? (Financial experts now recommend *not* depending on two incomes for regular living expenses, although many couples do.) Will the money coming in be his money and her money? Or will it be his *and* her money?

Think about spending attitudes and saving attitudes. Barb tells how **we** worked it out:

> Bob and I agreed that the money coming into our home would be *ours*. But like most couples we needed to determine if our physical needs could be taken care of with just one income. We decided in the very beginning that we would live on the income Bob made, however large or small, and in his student days it was pretty small. My income would be saved for "extras" and our future needs. (We knew instinctively that that was right for us, and now the experts are recommending it!)

> Then we had to decide which we wanted more, the additional money from an outside job for me, or the time gained if I became a full-time homemaker. It took a while for us to realize that that's what it is – a choice between money and time. If I had a job we'd have more money and could have a nicer car, bigger house, more elaborate vacation, and all the rest that more money can bring. But, obviously, if I had an outside job, our time at home would mostly be spent doing housework and other home-oriented chores. That would leave little extra time for ourselves, each other, or a family.

> However, if I was a homemaker, or worked only part-time, I could have most of the household chores done by the time Bob came home for the evening or for the weekend. We could have hired someone else to do those things (after our income grew) but then we'd have less money.

> We both wanted our children to have a full-time mother as they grew up, and we wanted free time for the fun things we like to do, both together and separately. So we chose to live with more

money and less free time until children entered our lives, and less money and more free time after our first child arrived.

Right from the start we accepted the fact that if we couldn't afford steak on Bob's income, we didn't *have* steak! But we *could* go for a walk together instead of doing the laundry or other household tasks, because we had *time* for a walk! For us that proved to be a good decision.

Bob adds:

A mutual decision about spending wasn't a problem for us, as it is with many couples. From the beginning we pretty much agreed on when to spend, which is whenever we need to, whether it's an emotional need or a material need, and when to save, which is whenever we can find unused money!

When our children had grown, it was time to re-evaluate and ask ourselves again, "Just how important is money in our relationship?" Bob continues:

In those days a large part of Barb's time was spent as a free-lance volunteer and on her business or her school work, all things which proved to be interesting and fulfilling, very life-giving. And we liked the flexibility we had by her not being obligated to an outside job or career. We could take vacations whenever I could fit it in – we didn't have to coordinate job schedules. And if I wanted to take an afternoon off, it could usually be worked out for both of us. So, for us, the decision for more time was still a good one.

In more recent years, our circumstances have changed again, as Bob points out:

I'm retired now, and quite honestly we've grown accustomed to living without expensive, unnecessary doodads and grown-up toys. So we need to discuss and decide once again how we want to divvy up the day. Do we want the additional time that retirement brings, so we can get going on the hobbies and volunteer work and the ever-mounting back-log of yard work we've postponed, or do we want the extra money that even occasional part-time jobs would bring?

Again, these things may seem unimportant to you now but they need to be discussed as they come up, and settled before either of you make assumptions that are wrong, and end up with big problems.

Decisions About Our Home

Should it be a house, a condo, an apartment, or maybe a mobile home? A house takes more maintenance than an apartment; who will take care of that? And what about the chores involved in keeping up any residence? Is the inside her responsibility and the outside his? As Bob says:

> Maintaining our home takes more time than either of us had ever expected, especially cars, appliances, and landscaping. Even for a small home. In our present home we deliberately put in low-maintenance landscaping, but even then it can eat up a full day or more each week if we always try to keep everything ship-shape.

These decisions about household responsibilities and chores are particularly difficult when both husband and wife work full time. There are many factors to consider, such as which one works longer, or harder, which one *likes* to do the various chores? The two of us see this area as a shared responsibility; in our home, the tasks are not mine or yours, they are *ours*; we each do what needs to be done. What will it be like in *your* home?

Decisions About Leisure Time

Early on, we discovered that, even with Barb at home, it's easy to have too little time for one another. Children, the house, recreation, and community service can quickly separate husbands and wives. As the children get older add *their* activities – soccer, dance class, PTA meetings, and on and on. And if both work full-time, it's even worse. It's important to choose some leisure time activities that support our marriage and draw us together, not pull us apart from each other. We both make it a point to spend time together, to enjoy each other and the relationship that we've developed.

Over the years we've *made* the extra effort to plan some recreation together, such as our couples club, a dance class, going out to plays or movies and out to dinner, even yard work. We made a definite effort to spend time together every day when Bob came home from work. We *enjoy* being together. For us, being together is very life-giving and nourishing for both of us.

Some of our leisure-time activities are *not* done together, though. Bob has taken some evening classes, has done some of the maintenance and held offices at church, and tutors English as a Second Language. Barb has been involved in volunteer work at our local hospital, was a wedding assistant at our church, has set up weekend retreats, has given Congressional tours (of the U.S. Capitol Building!), been an active Toastmaster, and played in a number of tennis leagues. Because we take the time to talk about our individual interests with each other, they haven't detracted from our marriage. Bob elaborates:

> The wide variety of Barb's activities has given her some unique experiences that make her a more interesting person. And her various landscaping projects have developed talents that we have taken advantage of for our own home.

Our leisure-time activities, whether separate or together, can enhance our marriage when they're not selfishly one-sided and when we share them with each other. We like to plan to spend time together, just as we did in our dating days. When we don't, we grow apart. It's automatic, because our priorities tend to shift. Each begins to feel lonely and separated. The same thing happens when we spend time together but don't communicate openly. What we need, what *every* married couple needs, is time, especially private time, to maintain and deepen our friendship. Taking time just for the two of us keeps us "turned on and tuned in" to each other.

Decisions About Sexual Activity

Couples should also make decisions, *conscious* decisions, about sexual activity, both before and after the marriage begins. Too often couples avoid actual discussion of this issue because of the reasons mentioned in earlier sections – inconvenient, uncomfortable, "peace at any price." But unless you've discussed it, how do you know that your behavior is what you both want? Follow the guidelines, just as with any other important decision, and consciously re-evaluate occasionally. This area requires openness as much as any other. How do you know that your fiancé hasn't settled for peace, at *any* price?

Decisions About Family Planning

There are many pros and cons about even *having* children, especially these days. Barb tells us:

> When I was younger, I was reluctant to discuss this area. I *wanted* a family with children; that seemed the best way to live. But I was scared. I'd never been a mother, and I wasn't sure I would do well at it. I liked taking care of my nieces and nephews, but being responsible for my own seemed like more than I was capable of. I didn't want to end up with a house full of bratty kids.

> Bob wanted children, too, and fortunately he had more confidence in our ability to raise them well. It also helped that he believed that child-rearing is the responsibility of *both* parents, not just the mother. That idea was not as popular then as it is today. Now, of course, I know that my fears were unfounded. But they were definitely very *real* fears.

We might not have been the best parents ever, but we managed to raise two beautiful daughters and we had a marvelous time doing it. Neither of us would trade parenthood for anything in the world –

we highly recommend it. (It leads to *grandparenthood*, and that's even better!)

There are as many demands as there are rewards in raising children. Of course, it isn't always easy – or cheap! Children are a big responsibility, and they're your responsibility for the first 18-20 years of their lives. They're a lot of work, they get sick, and they need to be disciplined, the things they need (and want) cost a lot of money, and they take a lot of time. But the fact is that they provide such fulfillment in return for the loving care that we give them. We can truthfully say that our lives and our marriage would be far less than they are if our children had not been a part of it. And it's even better as we grow older and our family increases with the addition of grandchildren.

There are *many* decisions to make in the area of family planning. We originally expected that we would have two or three children (at least one boy and one girl!), and by the time our second was about three years old, we realized that two was just right for us. Some couples today choose to remain childless. They want the freedom to spend their time and money in other ways, and a two-career couple can manage their time easier if there are no children. Of course that's a decision that *both* partners must make and it may have to be re-examined as time passes,

Decisions about birth control should also be mutual, and unselfish. There are several methods available: the pill, condoms, diaphragm, IUD (intra-uterine device, which we read recently is the most reliable and most widely-used) hormone capsule implants, the Billings method, natural family planning, abstinence, sterilization, or *no* artificial means. There are others, too, including some for men. They each have their risks, both in effectiveness and in safety. We recommend that you become familiar with all of these methods. Your doctor or books from the library or pamphlets from government agencies can give you written comparisons for the various methods. Then mutually decide which is best for your beliefs and your plans. *Not* to decide on a method of birth control is a decision, too, and that's okay, if that's what you *want*. Your decision should bring forth the best in you both. And remember that conditions and situations change, attitudes change. Re-evaluate your decision every once in a while.

What if conception is impossible? We never had to face the possibility of being unable to conceive a child, but we know that it can be a very real problem for some couples, a source of tension. Tenderness and acceptance are what's needed, not blame or feelings of inadequacy or guilt. It's best to discuss now, before it occurs, what your general attitudes are on the options that are available. What are your thoughts and how do you feel about such possibilities as adoption or foster-parenthood, or any of the medical options for artificial conception, or perhaps remaining childless? Just discuss *attitudes* now so that you each have an idea of what is going on in the other's mind. An actual decision will probably never be necessary because only a small percentage of couples cannot conceive – but it *might* be you!

We experienced the opposite extreme of inability to conceive – we had an unplanned conception! In Barb's words:

> To be honest, I was frightened. And immature. I was 20 years old at the time, and I selfishly thought that becoming pregnant at that time was spoiling our plans.

We were well aware, though (as we hope *you* are), that <u>no</u> method of birth control is 100% effective except abstinence and sterilization. Since we were both young and newly married, we weren't ready for either of those. It was a good time to remember that God has a plan for us and although it might be different from what *we* had planned for our lives just then, He does know what's best for us. Barb admits:

> I was wrong! Our baby girl was a delight, and she still is! Our plans weren't *spoiled*; they were merely changed.

Our second pregnancy wasn't exactly "planned" either, although we were ready for another child. And by this time our adorable daughter had shown us the joys of parenthood, so the news that we were about to have an addition to our family was very welcome. We realized that "unexpected" or "unplanned" does not necessarily mean "unwanted." (Our second daughter was, and still is, just as delightful!)

Discuss now, before it happens, your attitude toward an unexpected pregnancy, or if complications occur during pregnancy. How would you prefer to handle it? What would be most life-giving to both of you? To the baby? Don't make a decision yet, of course, but do discuss attitudes.

Decisions Regarding Our Relationships with Others

This is another big area for decision-making, especially with our parents. Often parents use the wedding as their last fling at exercising parental authority, particularly if *they* are paying for it. Considering that they've usually devoted about 20 years of their lives, their energy, and their money to nurturing us, it's not unreasonable to extend a little extra loving toward them at this time. Although it's *your* wedding, it's a very important event in *their* lives, too. It marks the end of their parental responsibility for you. It's a difficult time because even though the responsibility is over, it isn't the end of their love and caring. (It might mean a change in their lifestyle, too, so be easy on them.)

Ultimately, though, whether we're getting married or not, we must become fully mature adults and be independent of our parents. That means we set our own priorities and live our own lives – and we **accept responsibility for our decisions and actions**. Unless we *are* ready and willing to accept adult responsibility for our own behavior, we're not ready to be married. But making our own decisions doesn't mean that we reject our family background or our parents, or that we stop loving or being loved by them, or stop using their experience and advice if it's appropriate when making our decisions. They're often the best authority for us. But they should be advisors only. The actual *decision* should be ours.

Being married also means that when an irreconcilable conflict develops between our spouse and our parents, we must remember that our first loyalty lies with our spouse. This is hard for some young marrieds (and sometimes for their parents) to understand and accept. So we turn to the Bible for guidance, a good source of advice on most topics. (It doesn't cover *every* situation clearly but it covers a lot, and it's usually right!) And Holy Scriptures are very clear on this. In several places (Genesis, Matthew, Ephesians) we're told that "a man should leave his father and mother and be forever united to his wife." That goes for women, too, of course. Again, that doesn't mean rejection of parents. It means that loyalty to spouse comes *first.*

An example of this occurred early in our marriage. Shortly after our first child was born, when we lived close to Bob's parents, it developed that his mother was inclined to give advice when it hadn't been requested. In those circumstances, the advice was easy to interpret as criticism, although in retrospect it's doubtful that it was intended that way. Nevertheless, that's how it came across, and consequently, for a time the relationship with them became rather remote. It was no longer warm, close, and mutually supportive, as it had been. About that time Bob received a job offer that required us to move to another area of the country. Being at odds with his parents just then complicated the decision, and we knew they might assume that we were leaving because of the rift between us and them. But this was our future at stake, and it was obvious that accepting the offer was in our best interests. After we moved away, Barb made a point to write newsy letters to them every week. We know they treasured those letters. Making them a part of our lives and us a part of theirs, despite the differences of opinion, was a life-giving, loving decision.

Friendships outside our marriage and family also require decisions. We need to search out friends who will support our marriage. Both our individual friends and our friends as a couple must be people who want to see us stay together. We must make it clear to our friends and family that our marriage relationship comes first, and have the courage to avoid those who tend to draw us apart from each other. Having friends who oppose or ridicule marriage is going to have a bad effect on our marriage. We naturally evolved our circles of friends to include more and more married couples who liked *their* marriages.

Our Relationship to God

This area of decision-making also involves, for us and for any Christian couple, our belief in God. Even those of you who have no religious background whatever need to examine your beliefs and feelings about God — it's part of knowing yourself, exploring what's deep inside you. Some people believe in God, or *some* supreme being, and let it go at that. Others think about God a lot, and find God to be present, loving, and forgiving. Some people see God as a judge, with punishment for those who sin and special blessings and gifts for those who do good deeds.

How do *you* see God? Do you look to God in time of trouble? Is God close enough to hear or to care? Are you saved? If so, what are you saved from, and how? These are important questions for all of us to think about. Ask yourself, is my decision about God and church life-giving for me? And for us as a couple? Make two decisions, one for yourself and one mutually as a couple.

Just as many of you will have, the two of us together have a relationship with God also. Even before we married, we worshipped together, and we still do. It's like a habit, a *comfortable* habit. Without the habit we might feel reluctant or embarrassed about deciding to attend a worship service or some other function of our congregation. We know couples who *stay away* as a matter of habit. They miss out on regular exposure to God's messages and many of the other blessings of Christianity, such as a loving community of friends, and the nurturing that is there for us. Our decision to be regular in our worship has strengthened and enriched us as individuals and us as a married couple. Your decision can do the same for you.

Another life-giving decision we made in this area concerns spreading God's love through our involvement with engaged couples. As you know (if you read the first part of this book), we've worked "behind the scenes" and given talks on Engaged Encounter weekends, we've developed and presented a one-day program called ONE IN CHRIST for couples who couldn't afford either the time or money for a full weekend, and we've created this guidebook for couples who don't have access to either of those programs. All of these projects have been very helpful to others, and strengthened our own marriage. In the process we've both learned more about what makes marriage work and we've developed talents we didn't even know we had! We've volunteered our time and our money – and we've gained far more than money could match. That's what a life-giving attitude in just this one area has done for us. It can do as much for you.

One More Important Note

Number 3 of our guidelines for decision-making is the strong recommendation that all decisions be made mutually. That's often easier said than done. We've been asked "What do you do if you can't agree?" Agreeing to disagree is okay sometimes. But what if a decision must be made? What do you do? How to handle it? Let's say we have a situation where the wife has a very good job, and the husband gets a very good job offer in another state. A decision must be made one way or the other, to accept the job offer or to reject it. What do they do if they can't come to a mutual agreement? The answer to that question, too, can be found in the Bible. (Most answers are there, in one way or another; we're usually just too narrow-minded, or closed-minded, to heed the advice, especially when we disagree with it!) In Ephesians, Chapter 5, we read:

> "Honor Christ by submitting to each other. You wives must submit to your husband's leadership in the same way you submit to the Lord."

> "And you husbands, show the same kind of love to your wives as Christ showed to the church when he died for her."

Take it as a whole, not one part or the other. Men like to remember the part that says "wives submit to your husbands," but even earlier in the text it says that they should submit to each other, and if we continue on we read "… you husbands, show the same kind of love as Christ showed to the church…" He gave His *life* to take care of us!

A book we read a while back, and still refer to and highly recommend, *I Want My Marriage to be Better,* was written by Henry Brandt. In Chapter 6 he says that in any situation where two or more people must cooperate, a leader is necessary. Dr. Brandt goes on to say that we begin with cooperation, of course; we're partners, not opponents. But when final opinions still differ, and there must be a decision, there is no other way to settle it; a *leader* is necessary.

In the Christian family, the responsibility of leadership is the husband's, as the verse from Ephesians makes clear:

> "You wives must submit to your husband's leadership…"

Note that it does *not* say "submit to your husband's authority" nor does it say to submit to his demands. It says "submit to his leadership."

So what does this mean in today's terms? How do we handle it and still live peacefully in this era of equality between the sexes? It *is* possible! First, discuss the subject thoroughly. Husband and wife each give their viewpoint, opinion, and feelings, then come to a mutual decision. Obviously then, the husband would do what they have agreed upon. Neither the husband nor the wife should *always* be the one to give in – that becomes subservience or maybe "peace at any price" and neither of those is good for a relationship. The Bible verse above *begins* with the admonition to submit to *each other.* Neither one is to dominate.

If a decision cannot be reached and one *must* be reached, the husband is to take the responsibility of deciding. He has the obligation to determine what is best for all, not just look out for his own interests. (Ephesians 5:33 tells us "...a man must love his wife as a part of himself.") The wife is to respect his decision, trusting his judgment in determining what is best for them. (Again, in Ephesians 5:33 "...the wife must see to it that she deeply respects her husband...") If she really *can't* accept it (maybe sees it as unwise, unsafe, or even harmful) then more discussion is obviously needed. Also, they each need to decide if having their own way is more important than the quality of their relationship.

But to get back to the earlier example, what to do about this job offer? We've developed a system that works well for us. When we see that we have a difference of opinion, we each mull it over on our own, each thinking out a reasonable, fair solution. Then, for this situation, we'd get together and discuss the pros and cons of accepting the job offer, then discuss the pros and cons of staying, as suggested in guideline No. 2. We'd consider alternatives in either event: is it likely that Bob could get another offer as good in this area? Is it likely that Barb could get as good a job there? Are there other factors to consider? (closer or further from families, previous agreements we might have made with each other, other new opportunities, etc.) We'd try hard to come to a mutual decision. If that isn't happening, perhaps a compromise can be worked out: i.e., try it for a year or two, and then reconsider. As a last resort, Bob might have to make the decision on the basis of how Barb would accept his way versus how he could accept her way, keeping in mind that his decision must be what is best for both of us (and perhaps our children).

In this case, we *have to* come to a single decision because the only alternative here is separation, probably both emotionally and geographically. And neither of us wants that, neither is willing to accept that. Remember the wisdom above from Henry Brandt: A leader is needed whenever two or more people must cooperate. And in a Christian family the ultimate leader is the husband, even when his leadership determines that the *wife* should make the decision.

SUMMARY

This chapter, too, has contained a mountain of information. You probably learned a new term: life-giving. It means to be supportive, nurturing, and loving toward others, with a totally unselfish attitude. We gave suggestions on how to make wise decisions: pray for guidance, get all the facts, discuss and decide together, then periodically re-evaluate. We discussed some of the many decisions in marriage: relationship with each other, work, home, sex, family planning, time, our relationships with parents, relatives, friends, and with God. We finished up with a reminder of the Biblically recommended method for coming to a decision when husband and wife cannot agree.

Our goal in marriage is to love each other unconditionally, by living in a life-giving, nurturing, supportive manner. We think you'll find, as we have, that the best decisions are mutual, made in an unselfish way.

Notice that on this "Reflection" sheet there are a few ideas at the bottom that are specifically for those of you who are going into a second marriage.

Reflections #7

(20 minutes minimum for writing,
15 minutes minimum for discussion)

1. I am life-giving when I …
2. I (like/dislike) the decision-making process presented here because…
3. Major decisions we need to make include …
4. Decisions about career that we'll have to make include …
5. Tasks I will be doing around the house include …
6. How do I feel about the wife putting a career "on hold" to raise a child?
7. I (want/don't want) both of us to work full time because …
   Or
   I (want/don't want) one of us to be home with our children because …
8. Something I would like to discuss about our sexual activity is…
9. How do I feel about our decision about premarital sex?
10. I (want/don't want) children because …
11. I will be ready to accept the responsibility for raising a child when …
12. The birth control method I want to use is …
13. If we conceive a child before I think we're ready I think we should…
14. If we can't conceive when we're ready we should…
15. I plan to spend leisure time …
16. Activities I expect to do without you include …
17. I know I'm ready to be totally independent from my parents because…
18. The friends that will support our commitment to each other include…
19. In my relationship with God, I see Him as…
20. I felt particularly close to God when…

If this is not your first marriage:

- Decisions that need to be made regarding a former spouse include…
- How do I see (my/your) relationship to (your/my) children?
- Decisions that we need to make regarding the children include…
- We can make our family a unit by …

8

Yours, Mine, or Ours?
Managing Money in Marriage

As you no doubt know by now, finances play a big role in our lives and can create tension and discord between husband and wife. In fact, experts say it's the biggest single problem area in marriage. Not in-laws, not sex, but money! So it's important to learn how to handle it wisely, and to make *mutual*, life-giving decisions about managing money in a marriage. It becomes even more important to make mutual decisions in a two-career marriage. The first decision might be whether the money I earn is "mine" or "ours."

Communication Is Important

Before your marriage begins, we recommend that you discuss attitudes and feelings about the importance of money. Some questions to ask yourselves, to clarify your own attitudes:

- How important is money to me?
- What do my spending habits say about me? ...about my values?
  - Do I spend just to spend? Why?
  - Do I spend just to impress others? Do I need to?
- Will my wages be *my* money or *our* money?
- How do I feel about my spouse earning more than I do?

- How do I feel about friends/neighbors earning more than I do?

We need to continually keep each other aware of our desires, our needs, and our plans for our money because these things are continually changing. We ran into trouble in that area some time ago when Bob made a generous donation for a group-gift for a friend's anniversary. It happened at about the same time that Barb had purchased a very nice personal gift from just the two of us for the same friends! Either of those expenses would have been acceptable to the other, but we were both surprised at what our lack of communication did to our checking account!

Financial Decisions

The decisions regarding money need to be made mutually, just like the other decisions in marriage. Remember the steps:

- Prayer
- Getting the facts
- Discussion and mutual agreement
- Evaluation

Most couples make decisions on money matters even before marriage. One of the first items we shared a financial decision on was our wedding. (Until then we'd each made decisions on our own, without consulting the other.) Since Barb had been paying her own way for about two years by then, it never occurred to us that our wedding should be her parents' expense. We expected to pay for it ourselves, so we planned a very simple occasion, one that wouldn't put us in the poor-house. Our honeymoon, too, was at our own expense and again very modest. We'd heard stories of young couples who overspent for their honeymoon – and then lived on credit or welfare when they got back home! We didn't want that! So together we planned our expenses carefully.

Another decision might be called for when we're offered a substantial gift from parents or grandparents or a rich uncle. Do we accept? There are a number of things to discuss here before making this decision. Are there strings attached? How will each of us feel about taking the gift? Will we feel obligated to pay it back or reciprocate? How will the other person's family feel if they can't match it?

Then there's the everyday variety of financial decisions such as who will actually pay our bills. (Barb read that in 75% of the U.S. households women write the checks, regardless of which one earns more.) Another biggie, who will balance the checkbook? Barb tells what *we* did:

> We tried several different methods with this problem: each of us carrying a loose check, using two checkbooks with one account, using two separate accounts. None of those worked very well. We finally settled on one account and one checkbook, and eventually I ended up taking most of the responsibility. Not that Bob couldn't, but I seemed to get to it earlier than he (and I didn't mess up too often), so we just stayed with that. Bob wrote checks any time he needed to, but I usually had a better handle on what's what. Now that he's retired, he often gets to it before I do – now we both know clearly what's in our checking account. Usually.

You're probably very well aware of the different systems of handling money and when to use which. There's cash, checking account, debit cards, credit cards and buying on credit (financing with a formal loan). We know people who swear by each method and others who refuse to use each method. Obviously you need to discuss which you, as a couple, prefer – and, again, make a mutual decision.

Even though we're not financial experts, we will give you a very important piece of advice here. Whether you choose to buy on credit or not, we strongly recommend that you *establish* credit, in each of your names. Then, if you do run into a situation where you need a large loan (such as for a home or for a medical emergency), you'll find it easier to qualify because you have a credit history. You can establish credit by taking out a small loan, even if you don't need the money, and paying it back in regular installments. (Yes, it does cost you the interest to do it this way.) You can also establish credit by getting a charge card from Visa or MasterCard or any of the other major companies. Regular payment of these bills will give you a good credit rating, and if you pay them off in full each month it doesn't cost you anything, assuming you get a credit account with no annual fee. (Having a credit card is a requirement for renting a car, too.)

Another important financial consideration is savings. Discuss the value of having a nest egg for emergencies, or ready money to pay cash for cars or vacations or furniture. Is it important to you, or not? To both of *us* it's very important, so we've always had a savings account – not always big, but always there.

Remember that a charitable attitude and generous giving, are important to *all* levels of income, not just the rich or "those who can afford it," or limited to those who go to church. It includes *all* of us, and it includes giving to those who need our help, such as the American Cancer Society, Hospital Thrift Shop, the local soup kitchen or homeless shelter, and so many others. You don't have to give to all of them, of course, or to anyone and everyone who asks. Pick those that you think are deserving and give as you can. We've found that when we do, and do it lovingly, with no grudges, it has been a good thing, life-giving for both giver and receiver. Deliberately giving away part of our "wealth" on a regular basis prevents us from becoming too materialistic. And when we decide *together* how best to help others, we grow just a bit closer to each other.

Financial Planning

We've learned that, like generous giving, financial planning is important at all levels of income, too. At the lower level we call it budgeting and we tend to think of it as restricting, but that isn't quite so.

It turns out that we all manage better financially if we know our limits. We realized long ago that every couple, and actually every person, needs to recognize the difference between their "wants" and their actual "needs." Now that's become a more popular concept. We also had to learn to say, "I can't afford it." Those words are often hard to say, but each of us must, and we must each decide *when* we should say it. That "when" has changed for us over the years. The distinction between wants and needs is always the same, but as income increases we can afford to get more of the wants after the needs are taken are of. (We still can't afford everything – few people can!) Bob tells our experience:

> When we were on the lower income levels, we needed to plan just so we could make ends meet and pay our bills. As our income increased we found that we still benefited from planning because, when we did, the money left after our basic needs were met went as far as it possibly could. Planning also gave us a degree of flexibility that few people enjoy.

Even at a higher level of income, financial planning will help resist waste and careless spending, and to make intelligent use of the leftovers. This is important enough for the wealthy that they even pay others to help them do it. It's the same thing as budgeting but when you're rich, "financial planning" sounds better!

The questions of how to plan, what to include, how much in each category, and so on, will be answered differently for each of us. Talking to a financially wise friend or relative can be a good learning experience, too. And we recommend that you get a good book on financial planning. *It Only Hurts Between Paydays* by Amy Ross Mumford is an excellent one, and *The Financial Planning Workbook* by Larry Burkett is good. A book like this will give you the basic guidance you need with your plan.

One thing those books don't include, though, is this little-recognized bit of wisdom: how we spend our money often determines how we spend our time! If we buy a home, we should expect to spend the time to maintain a home, and that takes a *lot* of time. If we buy stocks, we'll probably spend our time following the progress of our chosen one. If we buy a boat, we should expect to go boating. Of course, we usually *want* to go boating if we buy a boat, but that's probably where we'll spend our time. We know people who feel they *must* go to their vacation home at least twice a month because they put so much money into it!

Remember to re-evaluate your financial plan, or budget, as time passes and circumstances change. For example, we spend a smaller fraction on recreation, food, and clothes now than we did when our children were growing up; we saved more when our income was at its peak and expenses were lower; and we invested more during those years. Now, with Bob retired, we have a whole new set of financial circumstances. Our golden years will be more comfortable for a longer period of time because we were wise enough to plan for it.

Three More Items Worth Mentioning

The first is insurance, and we won't say a whole lot about it. Again, we aren't experts here but we've learned some things from experience that we'd like to pass along. Insurance companies often try to sell us insurance that we don't always need nor can afford. When you buy insurance know what the policy covers and what it doesn't cover. The old saying is "The big print giveth and the small print taketh away" – **always read the small print.** That print isn't made small just so it will fit on one page! As Bob tells of his experience:

> I remember once, when I was young and naïve, being embarrassed about reading the fine print, and therefore obviously questioning the agent's word. I was afraid he'd think I didn't trust him. So I didn't read it – and I ended up buying a policy that I didn't understand and that we really couldn't afford. We canceled that policy later, but we lost the money we'd already put into it, which was several months' income.

We hope you don't make the same expensive, and foolish, mistake. Read before you buy. Again, talk to a knowledgeable friend or relative about what kinds of insurance are appropriate for your situation. Talk to several so you'll have a good overall view of what you need and how much it should cost. *Then* contact an insurance agent. Most insurance agents can provide you with a wealth of information, too. You might contact two or three before you actually buy.

Another very important item is a will, the kind that leaves stuff to people when you die. We aren't experts here either, but we do know that if you *don't* have a written will when you die, the state will decide how to divvy up your belongings. Many people, particularly young singles and newly marrieds, think they don't own enough to bother with a will. But you probably own more than you think, when you total it all up. And chances are there's something very special among your belongings that you'd like to see handled in a particular way. So do prepare wills, one for each of you. According to Denis Clifford (author of *Nolo's Wills*, Nolo Press) your will does not have to be drawn up by an attorney, but it should be typewritten or computer-printed. Handwritten wills are not valid in some states and often hard to prove legitimate so he doesn't recommend them. He adds that the fill-in-the-blanks form is legal in only four states, a video will is not legal in any state, and that an oral will is acceptable only under special circumstances in a few states. Whichever you choose, one drawn up by an attorney or one you prepare yourself, **do it**. The most important provision in your will could be naming the legal guardian for your children, if neither of you can care for them.

The third important item to consider is a Durable Power of Attorney, a document that states your wishes for your continued care if you aren't able to make that decision at the time it's needed. Without it you might spend years of your life in a coma (due to a serious accident or illness) in a nursing care facility. That's okay, if that's what *you* want, but the decision should be yours. You can get forms from any hospital or from a stationery store, and they must be notarized to be binding. Husband and wife each need one.

SUMMARY

Obviously, it's important that couples learn early in their marriage how to manage money wisely:

- It's the only sensible way to improve your lifestyle.
- Continual communication of wants, needs, and plans is vital.
- *All* the many financial decisions should be mutual decisions.
- Financial planning helps get the most from the money you have.
- Generosity toward those who need help almost always pays off.
- Include insurance and wills in your planning.

The challenge of money management never ends, we've found out. Remember that an unselfish attitude of handling whatever we earn can help us keep money and finances in perspective, and help us realize that there's more to life than the accumulation of possessions. Again, talking to a financially wise parent or friend as you draw up your plan can be a real learning experience. The *decisions* should be yours, of course, but they shouldn't be made in ignorance.

As you move on to the "Reflections" note that this sheet, too, has thought-provoking suggestions for those going into a second marriage.

Reflections #8

(Writing time 15 minutes, 15 minutes for discussion)

1. I want you/me to handle the finances because …
2. I think expenses for our wedding and honeymoon should be…
3. I want a high standard of living (and payments) because…
   OR
   I want a simpler lifestyle, buying as we can afford, because …
4. I (want/don't want) to start a "nest egg" right away because …
5. I (do/don't) want to use credit cards because …
6. My feelings about accepting money or gifts from parents are…
7. I (want/don't want) to include charities in our budget because …
8. I think we should talk to about our insurance needs because…
9. My thoughts about writing a will at this time are …
10. To me, the difference between "wants" and "needs" is…
11. My needs include …
12. My wants include …
13. My thoughts about financial planning and budgeting are …
14. I (do/don't) spend just to spend, or to impress my friends because …
15. My attitude about money is similar to yours in that …
16. My attitude about money is different from yours in that …

———

If this is not your first marriage:

- Financial obligations stemming from my previous marriage include …
- My obligations might affect our relationship because …
- My obligations might affect our lifestyle because …
- Knowing this, I feel …
- Knowing your financial obligations, I feel …

"We make a living by what we get. We make a life by what we give."

— Winston Churchill

9

Making Love?
Or Just Having Sex?

ex is part of our overall marriage relationship – it can be the most intimate form of communication. It isn't meant to be an isolated activity, as movies, TV, and songs like to promote. Sexuality is a God-given gift, to be shared between a married couple in a life-giving and responsible manner. (If you want verification of that, check 1 Thessalonians 4:3 and Hebrews 13:4. For those of you who are not Bible-readers, try it; at least for *this* standard. If you don't own a Bible, go to a bookstore to look up these passages. Paperback Bibles are not expensive.)

You probably think you know a lot about sex and don't need to read this chapter. After all, you're adults and you've had sex education in schools and you've "been around the block." Well, skip it if you want to. But when we've given this section in workshops almost every couple, young and old, naïve and experienced, has indicated that they learned something, including a medical doctor who thanked us for it! So we expect that *you'll* learn something, too. Maybe not from us – it might be from your fiancé, or it might be from within yourself.

Sexuality

God has given us the gift of sexuality. We read in Genesis 1:27-28, as a part of the story of creation, that the male and female which He created are to "be fruitful and multiply," and later, Genesis 2:24, still the story of creation, that "the two shall be one flesh," and in 1 Corinthians 7:3 that "The husband should give to his wife her conjugal rights, and likewise the wife to her husband." We could go on, but we just want you to realize that sexuality isn't something discovered by your generation, or ours, or Sigmund Freud, or Masters and Johnson, or the raunchy X-rated magazines, or any of the contemporaries. Exploited, maybe, but not discovered.

Sexuality is an integral part of every person. Sexual awareness and feelings are part of our daily life. Some of us may feel it stronger than others, but it does affect us all; it's a natural part of being human. And it isn't limited to intercourse.

Going back to the quotes above from Genesis, "the two shall become one flesh," and "be fruitful and multiply," and in Deuteronomy 24:5, where we are told to enjoy each other, we know that God intended sex for enjoyment, not guilt. The fact is, though, many people do experience uncertainty and guilt feelings. That's especially true when sexual intercourse occurs outside marriage. Even those who have abstained from having sex before marriage sometimes have a hard time changing from controlling their passion for each other to suddenly releasing that control with no feeling of guilt. But God's plan is for us to express love and receive pleasure in the intimacy of marriage through sex. Pleasures, joys, and gratification from sexual communication are natural and normal in marriage.

Marriage allows the most intimate sexual communication to develop. Unconditional love and our commitment to each other are important parts of this sensitive area of life.

Sexuality in Marriage

Like most people, both of us have attitudes about sexuality which developed over a long period of time, from our two different growing-up environments. Bob's experience is probably typical for men of his era:

> In my early years I was introduced to the dirty joke. Sex became known as something to be done for the men's benefit only, something men did to women. It was pure exploitation. Marriage and feelings of love were not mentioned.
>
> The same attitude prevailed among the friends I had in college, but it was supplemented with Playboy magazine. By Playboy's standards, sex was/is merely a physical act; it didn't involve love at all, and the possibility of sex *within marriage* was never mentioned.

Things haven't changed all that much in the intervening years, have they? Except that now many women are more willing to cooperate – some initiate it and some even demand it! And now schools teach sex education, the scientific basics; they're afraid to provide a moral viewpoint for fear of offending some parents. Magazines, TV, movies, and wild friends tend to emphasize an amoral, immoral, or exploitive viewpoint. Although they usually call it "making love," they rarely mention real love, the emotional connection; they're talking about nothing more than the physical act. And that's only because it makes *them* feel good – *they* love it! There's usually very little regard for their sexual partner, nothing that even comes close to *love*. Fortunately, there are many good books on sexual activity within the bonds of marriage and we recommend that you get some of these (more than one, for sure) and we can almost guarantee that you'll learn from them and that you'll like what you learn.

It's important to our sexual relationship to maintain an air of romance in our *total* relationship. We should each give our love-life high priority, but not as an isolated act of sex – it should be a part of the total relationship. Sexuality is a part of our *daily* love life, not just when we hop into bed together. Candles, soft music, a gentle kiss or touch, phone calls at work, love notes. These are all ways to keep romance in our relationship, ways to focus on each other. Barb gives a specific example:

> When Bob went on a business trip he often hid love-notes for me. A while back I found one as I stepped into the shower. It read, "I like your outfit!

We've found that our sexual relationship is a progressive one that deepens with the growth of the total relationship.

Your Honeymoon

This is where your sexual relationship as husband and wife begins. The wedding day is usually a hectic, busy time and both the bride and the groom are usually very tired, both emotionally and physically drained. We urge you to plan a honeymoon that's relaxing so that you can enjoy each other. Bob remembers:

> Our honeymoon was very low-key. We had friends who went to a secluded cabin in the northern part of the state, and others who'd gone to more exotic places, but... We were living in Milwaukee then, so we planned a leisurely week in Chicago, thinking that if we really got bored with each other there would be plenty of museums and other attractions to visit!

Now, we don't necessarily recommend that you spend your honeymoon in Chicago, but we know that a relaxed and leisurely honeymoon is by far the most enjoyable. You'll have many years and many opportunities to do the more elaborate things, as we have. Take *this* time to concentrate on each other.

Wherever you choose to spend your honeymoon, try not to be uptight and intent on making it perfect. Stay loose, laugh at the funny things that happen. Some friends of ours chose to go camping on their honeymoon, and they stuck to their plans even though it was raining. To Barb that was funny enough, a honeymoon camping in the rain (Barb is **not** a camper). But the really funny part came after they had put up their new tent and were all settled in for the night. After a little while they got down to the business of "honeymooning." They became so involved with each other and so oblivious to their surroundings that, well – they broke the tent pole! Their romantic escapade was interrupted most abruptly. They ended up with a collapsed tent, in the rain, in the middle of the night! The next day they tried to explain to the other campers what all the commotion during the night had been about, but since everyone knew they were honeymooners, they just nodded knowingly! Our own honeymoon brings back humorous memories, too. In Bob's words:

> We woke up that first morning as husband and wife and were both ecstatic. Like most newlyweds, we'd been exhausted by the time we reached the hotel on our wedding night, but in the morning we couldn't get enough of each other – we learned the true meaning of "breakfast in bed!" I remember the staff at the hotel dining room just loved our asking for the breakfast menu at 2 p.m.!

So if something like that happens, try to be relaxed enough to laugh at it then, because you surely will laugh in the coming years.

Good sexual communication, too, needs openness and a willingness to be vulnerable. It continues throughout marriage. If either of you are anxious or in a hurry, let the other know your feelings. We've heard it said that "a man is like a light bulb; flip a switch and he's turned on. But a woman is more like an iron; it takes longer for her to get hot, and then takes a while for her to cool down!" Or to put it another way, most women need 15-30 minutes of foreplay for arousal and are best aroused by tenderness and touch, whereas most men need much less time and generally tend to be easily stimulated visually. That's what the experts say, anyway. Different people react differently, of course, and you need to communicate *your* preferences. But we do suggest that you slow down; savor the time with each other. A love relationship calls us to nurture the ego of our marriage partner. Take the time to do that, be sensitive to each other's needs. Honest communication on what satisfies leads to fulfillment and true love-making, rather than just sexual activity.

Lovemaking

Surprise! This section is short, because there are a number of authors who are much, **much** better than we at giving you the information you need here. One of our favorite books is *The Act of Marriage* by Tim LaHaye. It was first written many years ago, but it's been up-dated several times and it's still good.

We *will* tell you that married couples need to strive to **make each other the focus** of lovemaking, not just to satisfy our own passion. When sex becomes selfish and self-centered, it isn't life-giving; sometimes it isn't even pleasurable. It's no longer an expression of love – it's just **sex!** A good sexual relationship is based on giving, not on getting. And another thing, sex shouldn't be used as a weapon or as a reward; it's meant to be a shared experience, done with, not to, a spouse. It should be *love making*, building the love between the two of you.

Family Planning

Any discussion of sexuality and sexual activity should naturally include a section on family planning – it should probably come first! As mature and responsible adults, you're probably already aware that *any* time a normally healthy male and female engage in sexual intercourse there's a possibility that a new life will be created. By now you know that the *only* 100% sure way to avoid pregnancy is to either not have sexual intercourse or if one is physically incapable of conceiving. Some artificial birth control methods are very effective, but none of them are totally reliable.

You understand then that it's important to make responsible life-giving decisions in the area of family planning. We talked earlier about various methods of contraception and we want to stress here that contraception is a *mutual* responsibility. If we don't want to conceive a child, we're *both* responsible if conception occurs despite our efforts.

How Pregnancy Affects the Sexual Relationship

Sexual activity during pregnancy can be affected by many different things. It may continue as before conception until the bulk of the baby makes it physically uncomfortable. But in many cases a woman's desire for sex may increase or decrease at various stages of the pregnancy. Barb tells her experience:

> In the early months I found that I was much too sleepy for sex at night. Until then I didn't know that pregnancy can make women sleepy – *very* sleepy. For a while, since we were both at work during the day, sex had to be limited to weekends.

Honest communication is vital during this time, and the decision to make love should be mutual. (When it isn't mutual, it's just sex!) Physical difficulties or medical problems may rule out sexual intercourse during part of a pregnancy, but the need for tenderness and affection remains, for both the husband and the wife. It's part of sexuality. Maintain the romance, keeping the focus on each other, and remember that making love doesn't always have to result in intercourse.

When Barb became pregnant we had a good medical doctor but he was useless as an advisor to prospective fathers, and Bob admits that he was too embarrassed to ask for advice. He didn't even know what to ask! Don't let that happen to you! There's a lot written now on what to expect during pregnancy. We urge you, when the time comes, to read up on what's happening and talk to your doctor – together. Take your list of questions along. Read some books together before you go to the doctor, so you'll understand what's going on and what he/she is talking about. One book that we've heard recommended by a number of young couples is *What to Expect When*

You're Expecting by Arlene Eisenberg, Heidi Murkoff, and Sandee Hathaway. (It's part of a series and we've heard that the whole series is very good – check it out.) Know as much as you can about what's happening – to her body and to your relationship. Bob recalls:

> As Barb's body was getting ready to present the world with our daughter, there were some pretty obvious changes. We expected the visible physical changes, of course. But the hormone changes! Hormones bring on the visible changes, but they influence moods and emotions, too. Barb had periods of sadness, of anxiety, lack of confidence in herself. Other times she was unusually serene or very ambitious. These mood changes were as real and as valid as the physical changes, but they were harder to predict and hard to understand.

And they can be much harder to accept if we don't know about them ahead of time. It's worth the time it takes to learn all you can about *all* the hormonal changes that take place during pregnancy.

Only the wife can fully experience pregnancy and childbirth, but both husband and wife have a shared responsibility during this time. It's as good a time as ever to love and cherish one another, and it may be even more important than at other times. Bob didn't get to witness the births of our daughters; it wasn't allowed back then. Things are different now. We encourage husbands to be there, to hold her hand, to help with the delivery if possible, and to begin bonding with the infant. It helps their marital relationship if he knows what's going on during the birth of his babies. Bob was nearby, but he wasn't in the delivery room. It was a unique time of special emotional closeness for us, but we know that it could have been even better.

After childbirth sexual activity can be a frustrating time. As Barb remembers:

> We yearned to fully express our deepened love for one another. But our doctors, in both cases, told us very clearly not to have sexual intercourse until after my six-week check-up. That wasn't

what we wanted to hear, but we decided that my health and safety were more important than satisfying our sexual urges. We were glad that we'd learned to control those urges before our marriage began; we knew that we could again.

We needed to keep in mind, too, that new parents are in a new situation and that there might be both physical and emotional changes from pre-baby days. So there was a need to approach this new relationship with openness, love, and acceptance.

SUMMARY

Recognize and acknowledge that sexuality is a gift from God, an integral part of every person, all day, every day, given for us to express our love and receive physical pleasure in the intimacy of marriage. Our sexual relationship as a married couple is a progressive one that deepens along with the total relationship. Good sexual communication continues throughout marriage, not just during courtship or the early years of marriage. Lovemaking is most satisfying for both of us when we focus on pleasing our spouse.

Sex is a natural part of our lives. Marriage between a man and a woman allows that part of our selves to nurture our overall relationship. It shouldn't become the total focus of our life, and it shouldn't be ignored either. Our sexual relationship is more than sexual intercourse. All physical contact doesn't have to lead to sexual intercourse, and it won't. Each day we need affection, hugs, kisses, kind words; these are important and we need to be aware each day of the physical affection our spouse needs, even if it's just a touch or a kiss.

Family planning, remember, is the responsibility of both the husband and the wife. And remember that sexual activity will probably have to be adjusted during and after pregnancies.

Again you'll notice that these "Reflection" suggestions include ideas for those going into a second marriage.

Reflections # 9

(Minimum writing time is 15 minutes, 15 minutes for discussion)

1. The questions about sex that I most want to talk to you about are…
2. The attitudes about sex that I grew up with include…
3. My sex education comes basically from…
4. Regarding the physical details about sex, I'd like to learn more about…
5. The things that I find physically attractive about you include…
6. We can assure maximum sexual pleasure for both of us by…
7. The thing that concerns me most about our sexual relationship is…
8. My ideal honeymoon would be…
9. Some things I would like to do to "set the mood" include…
10. The sexual acts that I think are improper in marriage include…
11. To me, the difference between "having sex" and "making love" is…
12. I plan to maintain an air of romance in our total relationship by…
13. When I think about (you) being in the delivery room I feel…
14. If we found out that one of us couldn't have children I would feel…
15. Learning to control sexual urges before marriage brings feelings of…
16. Having to control sexual urges after the birth of a child is…

———

If this is not your first marriage:

- Our sexual relationship is/will be unique because…
- We can develop, build, and maintain our uniqueness by…
- I can let the past be past by…

- Knowing that you have had a sexual relationship with another person…
- Knowing that I have had a sexual relationship with another person…

"Love does not consist in gazing at each other, but in looking together in the same direction."

— Antoine de Sain-Exupery

10

You Want <u>SIX</u> Kids?
Setting Goals and Priorities

Experts say that it's a good idea to set goals – how else can you achieve anything in life? Well, we've never been big on formally setting goals and we've achieved quite a bit. No one can predict the future with certainty so sometimes, even with the best of intentions, planning and setting goals just doesn't work out. We do know that planning for the future and setting priorities *can* shape our lives, give us directions, and help us focus our lives. And we know that taking the time to plan together can bring the two of us closer, because we're investing in one another's lives. We'll show you how to apply these ideas to *your* marriage.

Here's What <u>We</u> Did

Barb's story:

> Even before I met my future husband, I expected that I'd work for a few years, then marry a man who would eventually earn us a comfortable living. We wouldn't be rich, as such, but neither would we live from paycheck to paycheck. And I wanted to live in a warmer climate; the mid-west was too cold. California sounded good to me. When children entered the picture, I expected to quit my job and become a full-time homemaker, at least until our children were grown.

And Bob's:

> My plans after high school centered on a B.S. degree at the state university. Longer-range plans included marriage and a nice home in the city or suburbs, not a rural area. I expected my wife to be a full-time homemaker when we had children. I had expectations, but except for college, I really wasn't into goal-setting.

We didn't exactly shoot for the moon, did we? When we were first married, we really hadn't set *our* goals. At least not long-range goals. Shorter goals were much like yours probably are: set up a place to live and furnish it as nicely as we could afford. We knew that whatever long-term goals we did set would most likely cost money, so you could say that our first goal was to build our savings account. It wasn't a consciously-set goal, but we knew that we needed *some-thing* to aim for. If we had planned a little more specifically, we might have achieved more. But if we hadn't had even this vague goal, and the priorities toward attaining it, we could easily have wasted our money bit by bit on frivolous things and never really achieved any-thing! Planning helps us focus on the things in life that we think are important, and it gives us direction.

We learned, too, that goals change as life changes. As Barb recalls:

> A little over a year after we married, Bob went back to school, and we were on our way to student life. Since we had our first child by then and we wanted me to be at home with her, it meant very low income. We were glad that we'd had the forethought to build our savings, because we knew that we'd need it for living expenses while Bob was in school. So then our goal became graduation day.

While a graduation isn't a material goal, such as a house, car, or other possession, it *was* a goal, just as having a family or a particular use of our spare time can be non-material goals.

It's important for us to set realistic, achievable goals and to re-evaluate them periodically, to make sure that that's what we both still want. As the end of school neared, Bob was asked to consider continuing on to a higher degree. We discussed this suggestion and together we decided that this new goal was attainable and it was certainly worthwhile, so we changed our goal to a *different* graduation day.

Priorities Vs. Goals

Understand that goals and priorities are not the same thing. There's an important distinction. As we define them for this section, a goal is something we want to achieve eventually. To own a home, graduate from school, take a vacation to Hawaii – those are goals. A priority is how we choose to spend our time, our energy, and our money right now. Today. This week.

A priority for us has been to spend time together as a family and, even though our children are grown now, we often still make the extra effort, and sometimes the extra expense, to be a complete family whenever we can. Another priority is to spend some time together, just the two of us, to enrich our marriage and just enjoy each other.

Other priorities may be in the area of money – do we have something inexpensive like hotdogs on Monday so that we can see a movie on Tuesday? Do we save the unexpected windfall for a little sailboat – or do we spend it on a party for our friends?

Priorities are also evident in how we spend our time and energy. If a husband spends his time nights and weekends on a project at work, he'll have less time to spend with the family. If his priority is to ride his bike to work, he probably won't have the energy to do yard work or go for a walk with his wife in the evening.

As you can see, our priorities dictate how we spend our time, our money, and our energy. Our priorities can lead us to our goals – or they can prevent us from ever reaching them!

Common sense tells us that priorities and goals should be compatible. There's no point in setting a goal of owning a home if our priorities are to spend all our money on expensive boats, cars, and clothes instead. We like nice vacations. We don't have them very often, but when we do they're usually at picture-postcard resorts. With this in mind, we buy used cars and drive them until they beg to be replaced, and we wear our clothes until they're thread-bare or we've "outgrown" them. Thus, our goal, which is an occasional very nice vacation, influences our daily priorities. They are compatible. That makes sense, of course, but for some reason, unless we really think about it, we often don't <u>do</u> that.

Keep in mind that although it's often helpful to set goals and to keep priorities compatible with those goals, it's equally important to be flexible, to leave room for spontaneity and an occasional "irresistible opportunity." That happened to us while Bob was still in school. As he remembers:

> I was working day and night on my dissertation so I could finish as soon as possible, get out of school, and earn some big money. So, we didn't go out very often. But one afternoon an old friend, Tom, called. He was in the area for just a few hours and hoped that we could get together. Taking a night away from my school work would make our goal one day further away, but we decided to spend the evening with Tom.

We realized that we shouldn't be so rigid in following our life-plan that we miss out on all the fun!

Changes in Planning: From "My" Life to "Our" Life

When a man and woman decide to marry, it's time to adjust their individual goals and priorities to a *combined* set of goals and priorities. In Barb's words:

> I expected to marry and raise a family, so that didn't change. But my plans hadn't taken into consideration what my husband might want. We needed to sit down and discuss our dreams and

to determine where they differed. Fortunately, most of our goals blended smoothly – Bob's "home in the suburbs" fit very nicely with my hope for a warmer climate. Combined planning was easy for us.

There may be unspoken plans and priorities that need to be brought out into the open before joint goals are set. For example, if either plans to go to school, to move frequently as a career might require, to make regular visits to the parents, to start a family immediately or wait several years – the list goes on. These personal plans should be discussed before the goals for the marriage are set. Barb says:

> I knew that Bob had considered going back to school, but we never really discussed when, or what level of priority it held until his application was accepted and we *had* to make a decision. If I'd still been employed, I might have resented giving up my good job with a nice salary so that Bob could return to school in another part of the country. As it was, we had to determine if we *could* live on our savings plus his stipend until he graduated, and we also had to decide if we both *wanted* to change to a lower standard of living.

You can easily see that open discussion of plans should become an on-going process. We've never regretted our choice, but if we'd discussed our plans earlier, we would have avoided being forced into a quick decision that might have been the wrong one.

Any unspoken priorities should be brought out into the open. Even when a priority seems so obvious to one of us, an open discussion of plans is always a good idea. You can be sure that a husband's goals won't always be the same as a wife's and neither will priorities. So often, particularly during engagement but also during marriage, we can be tempted to assume that our fiancé or our new spouse will automatically agree with our plans. That can work, but don't count on it. You may each have plans that conflict with the other's. An engaged couple in one of our workshops provides a perfect example. She planned to work until their first baby arrived, then become a full-time homemaker, as her mother had done. Her fiancé, though, expected to buy a nice home for their new family, and he was counting on her salary to help pay the bills, the way his parents had done. Each had made assumptions, and the assumptions were not only wrong, they were incompatible. Prompted by our recommendation to compare their plans, they talked about this before their marriage began and came up with a compromise that both could live with. (Their solution was to adjust their spending so that they could save all of her salary until the baby came, then when the baby was four months old she went back to work part-time.)

Of course, we should expect to compromise. Even now, the two of us may have different goals and priorities and may each have to compromise. And occasionally there will be total sacrifice of what one of us wants. Bob remembers:

> There was one summer several years back when we were invited to spend a week at a friend's luxurious cabin in the mountains. It was going to be a relaxing and very enjoyable time and Barb really wanted to go. I wanted to go, too, but it wasn't a good time for me to be away from work. My priority right then was my job. So we discussed it and agreed to forget about the week at the cabin. We'd go another time.

But How Do We Really Do It?

Here's an example of how we've done this goal- and priority-setting, how *we* carried it out. One of our most important goals was set early in our marriage, one we still maintain: to stay out of debt. We knew we couldn't pay for a *home* outright, of course, but everything else was to be paid for in full, either on the spot or when the bill came at the end of the month. As mentioned earlier, neither of us liked the idea of paying high interest costs to purchase things we really couldn't afford at the moment. It just didn't seem right. Or wise. Besides, we could buy *more* if we didn't pay that money in interest. Setting the goal is only half the plan, though. To achieve and maintain that goal we had to set our priorities wisely. A priority that went along with this goal was that we'd have to watch our spending and keep it within our limits. (Within payable limits, not within our credit limits!) Together we discussed it, decided that the end result was what we both wanted, and agreed to do that.

Over the years this has worked very well for us and we recommend it. Living with no debts, free of financial burdens, has been a reward in itself. Even when we bought a new car, we waited until we had the money to pay cash. However, the dealer pointed out that if we bought the car with a special car loan, which came at low interest, then invested our lump sum in a higher-interest tax-free bond, we'd actually make money! So, we needed to re-evaluate our goal, to clarify just what it was that we both wanted. Bob remembers:

> It was true, we could make money by buying the car with a loan, so we did it. But as time went on, neither of us liked the idea of driving around in a car that belonged to someone else; the payments reminded us of that fact each month. So when it came time to make the third payment, we paid it off in full. We probably lost a little money on that whole deal, but the relief we felt was worth it.

We learned that, for us, time payments are not the way to live. This experience convinced us once again that we had made the right decision years ago. And an unexpected bonus was that our relationship was strengthened because of it.

SUMMARY

We hope you realize now, better than we did in the early years, the importance of planning, how it can help us focus our lives to determine what goals we want to achieve, and how it gives us direction to set us toward those goals. Good intentions are not enough. Understand the difference between goals and priorities: a goal is something you want to achieve; a priority is how you actually spend your time, money, and energy. The two must be compatible to be effective. Now that you're getting married, your planning should change from "mine" to "ours." Neither partner in a good marriage will always get his or her own way, of course, but remember that compromise and sacrifice are a normal part of marriage. Again, decisions on both goals and priorities should be mutual. Remember that even after plans are set, it's important to remain flexible. Unexpected opportunities happen.

Sitting down together to set realistic goals and the priorities that help us reach those goals will give us incentive to achieve far more than we otherwise would, while it deepens our relationship.

This next exercise will be to discuss *your* goals and priorities. Each of you will have two sheets, one each per person. Just follow the directions on the sheets. Complete the Goal-Setting first, then the Priority-Setting. Let your fiancé know now your hopes, dreams, and aspirations, for both of you as well as for yourself, and realize that each major goal should and perhaps must become a mutual one. Again, answer all of these, even if your fiancé already knows the answer. Also, we know that it's good to repeat an exercise like this every few years. Even the best plans require revision as circumstances change, and ideas or wants and needs change.

Reflections #10

(Minimum 20 minutes for the two exercises,
15 minutes total to discuss)

GOAL-SETTING

1. The major long-term (more than 2 years) goal in my life right now is…
2. My short-term (less than 2 years) goals include…
3. A goal I haven't mentioned to you yet is…
4. In five years: (circle the options that best apply)
   a. We will be living in a:
      house   mobile home   apartment   condo
      We will be: renting   buying
   b. We will have   0   1   2   3 _____ children
   c. I will be: employed   a student   at home
   d. You will be: employed   a student   at home
   e. Other goals we will have attained include…
   f. Other goals we'll be working toward include…
5. In ten years: (circle the options that best apply)
   a. We will be living in a:
      house   mobile home   apartment   condo
      We will be: renting   buying
   b. We will have   0   1   2   3 _____ children
   c. I will be: employed   a student   at home
   d. You will be: employed   a student   at home
   e. Other goals we will have attained include…
   f. Other goals we'll be working toward include…
6. A goal I have that seems more like an impossible dream is…

PRIORITY-SETTING

In order to plan your life and to set priorities, it's best to begin with the general pattern your life will probably take. Think of the lifestyle you desire. What are your priorities in the following areas?

1. Choosing how I *want to* use our time, this is how important these items are to me (not necessarily the amount of time spent, but *how important* they are):

   (Rank these 1 to 12, with 1 being the most important)

Work	Children
Church activity	Household duties
Hobbies	Worship
Recreation	Time together
Time alone	Relatives
Friends	Charity work

2. Choosing how I think we should use our money:

   (Rank 1-12, as above)

Food	Education
Personal	Recreation
Housing	Church
Insurance	Clothing
Savings/Investing	Charities
Cars	Other _____

3. My priorities (do/do not) lead to my goals because…

4. Re-do items 1 and 2, showing how I *actually* use my time and money.

5. The changes I need to make so that we can reach our goals include…

6. I (am/am not) willing to make those changes because…

11

I'm Sorry – Please Forgive Me
The Need for Forgiveness

In a lasting relationship there are bound to be times when one's action results in a hurt for the other. Whether the hurt is intentional or not, when there is hurt there's a need to forgive and to reconcile and heal. Forgiveness is the first step in the process that leads to reconciliation and healing. These three, forgiveness, reconciliation, and healing, are intertwined. They involve coming together after an emotional separation caused by hurts. They include discussion, sharing of feelings, and recognition of our own and each other's shortcomings. Sometimes the process is fast, perhaps only minutes. And sometimes it can be very slow, as in months. True forgiveness and reconciliation erase guilt feelings, mistrust, and hurt; those are replaced by feelings of inner peace, joy, greater love, and inner growth. And healing occurs.

The Reconciliation Process

We realized long ago that the people who hurt us the most and whom we hurt the most are those whom we love the most. We hurt because we care. For a married man or woman, our spouse is the premier example. The following passage from Colossians 3:12-14 talks about forgiveness:

"...practice tender-hearted mercy and kindness to others. Don't worry about making a good impression on them but be ready to suffer quietly and patiently. Be gentle and ready to forgive; never hold grudges. Remember, the Lord forgave you, so you must forgive others. Most of all, let love guide your life."

Sometimes a wife or husband, or both, get angry at each other and the anger often leads to an emotional separation and loneliness that neither really likes or wants. This passage from the Bible reminds us that if we will just forgive, and once again make the decision to love him or her, that separation and loneliness will go away. Of course, we don't always remember it in the heat of anger, but we do know that it's always true.

It's easy to understand the need for an apology, but when the hurt is caused unintentionally, it often seems unnecessary or even unreasonable to ask for forgiveness. Bob offers:

When I make a suggestion or maybe criticize something Barb has done, I usually do it to help her. However, sometimes her feelings are hurt. But I did it for her own good – I didn't mean to hurt her, so why should I apologize?

Why? Simply because it's the loving thing to do. But even that isn't enough.

To say "I'm sorry" is merely a statement, and that might be the end of it. Those words can come across as a casual "excuse me" or "oops!," sounding shallow and insincere. It doesn't explain the reason for the apology, and it doesn't invite a response.

It's far better to move into and through the healing process. After a sincere, specific apology, it's very important to take the next step, which is to add "Please forgive me." When forgiveness is asked, it's a request, inviting a response, and it turns the control of the hurt over to the one who has been hurt. Of course, when this is done, there's the risk of having the request rejected, and *not* being forgiven. It's a situation of personal vulnerability similar to what we talked about earlier.

A major barrier to asking for forgiveness is pride, or ego. Bob admits that:

It's especially difficult for me when I don't really believe, or maybe don't realize, that I've done wrong. I only know that Barb is hurting. It may be easier for me to give her a gift to try to make her feel better. Or maybe just hope she'll forget whatever it was I did, and let time heal the hurt.

But neither gifts nor hoping she'll forget works very well to ease the hurt. In fact, the hurt often deepens because we haven't cleared it up.

Pride can also interfere when it's time to *do* the forgiving. Forgiving can be difficult. Barb, too, admits that:

Sometimes I *want* Bob to know I'm hurting, to make sure he's aware of just how deeply he hurt me. Other times I realize that he doesn't know what he did to hurt me. Then I have to tell him, or the healing will never occur and the loneliness continues.

Note that we are not judging right or wrong of the action that caused the hurt; we are forgiving the hurt caused by the action. That's a very important distinction: **We're not judging the action; we're forgiving the hurt caused by the action.** To truly forgive means to say, "I accept and love you, without conditions." Then the reconciliation can occur and the healing of the hurt will begin. However, if the hurt feeling remains, true and complete forgiveness has probably not yet occurred.

From the other side, we should remember that unless we *accept* forgiveness, we'll continue to feel guilt for our wrong-doing. And similarly, if we continue to feel guilt, it's an indication that we haven't fully accepted forgiveness.

Notice that forgiveness heals both the one who is hurt and the one who caused the hurt. The emotional separation begins to disappear and the relationship is once again whole. Both win!

SUMMARY

As we summarize, remember that, as Christians, the Lord has forgiven us, so we are to forgive each other. We repeat that every time we say The Lord's Prayer:

> "...forgive us our trespasses as we forgive those who trespass against us..."

(For those of you who aren't familiar with this supplication, try it; it really does work.)

Realize that the forgiveness-reconciliation-healing process has several steps:

1. Apologize, being specific.
2. Ask for forgiveness.
3. Forgive.
4. Accept forgiveness.

Remember also that forgiveness heals both of us.

In a marriage relationship, because of the trust that develops, we are powerful in the way we hurt and just as powerful in the way we heal. The need for forgiveness in a love relationship is vital. Forgiveness allows us to go on loving and being loved.

Before going on to the "Reflection," take a moment now to consider if anything between you needs to be reconciled, any big or little hurts that you may have cause each other recently, particularly as you've been working on your marriage preparation. Consider also your wedding preparations. Reflect on the events of the past sessions, or the past week. Write down a hurt you may have caused and ask for forgiveness. Or maybe a hurt you have suffered. Be open to revealing that hurt and forgiving it. Remember that forgiveness is an essential part of the Christian faith; it's a good practice for people of other faiths or no faith, too.

Reflections on Forgiveness

(Minimum writing time 10 minutes; 10 minutes for discussion)

Take a moment to think if there is any emotional hurt that needs to be reconciled between the two of you. Any little hurt that you might have caused each other recently, today, this past week. This is not a time to confess your past sins, but to reconcile a hurt you might have caused. Simply ask yourself, "Have I caused my fiancé any hurt?" Write it down in your notebook. Then ask for forgiveness. Or perhaps you've *suffered* a hurt. Write it down. Reveal the hurt.

OR

Recall a recent emotional hurt. Did you forgive, or ask for forgiveness? If not, do it now. Describe the incident and how you felt about it. Write it in your notebook, along with your forgiveness or your request for forgiveness.

OR

Ask yourself, "How do I feel about the way we heal each other's hurts? How do I feel about asking for forgiveness? …about forgiving? Write your response in your notebook.

"A wedding is a day...
marriage is a lifetime."

– Engaged Encounter motto

12

The Vows to Last a Lifetime

Traditional, or contemporary?

Many people hear their marriage vows for the first time on their wedding day, each says their "I do" and they go on with the show. Afterward they have no idea what it was that they promised, until they see it on the video! Even then, many don't know what it *means* – it's just something you go through as part of the ceremony. Well, we've learned what it means, and in this chapter we'll tell *you*. We also want to explain what a betrothal is, how it's a manner of preparing for marriage, a deeper commitment than engagement. We'll clarify the difference between preparation for a wedding and preparation for a lifetime of marriage. And we'll encourage you to assess your readiness for marriage before going further. But we're getting ahead of ourselves. Let's back up a bit.

The Wedding Vows and What They Mean

The traditional wedding vows happen to be the vows we used in our wedding. We aren't saying that these are the vows that *you* have to use, but we'll use them here as a basis for what we're talking about. The traditional vow:

> "I, _____ take you, _____, to be my wedded wife/husband, to have and to hold from this day forward, for better, for

worse, for richer, for poorer, in sickness and in health, to love and to cherish, till death us do part, according to God's holy ordinance, and thereto I plight thee my troth."

But just what does this vow mean? How can we live out our wedding vows? We'll tell you how *we* understand it, how it was explained to *us*. Let's take it one part at a time. Bob begins:

"I take you, Barb, to be my wedded wife..."

This tells the world that I have chosen **Barb** to be my wife, of all the women in the world. I have made the decision to love her, and I want everyone to know it and to respect my decision.

"...to have and to hold..."

This does not mean that I own Barb, or plan to dominate her in any way. It means that I will support her in all ways, and strive to increase our closeness as our marriage progresses. She will be my intimate friend.

In marriage we touch each other emotionally, spiritually, and physically, as in no other relationship.

"...from this day forward..."

These words remind us of the on-going nature of our relationship, the part that makes it enduring. Bob continues:

Before our wedding day, we had become aware of our oneness, our unity, and on that special day we publicly and officially declared our life-long commitment to each other, with friends and family as witnesses. When our clergyman asked the BIG question, we didn't say "I do," meaning for now and as long as it's convenient and all goes well. It's easy to say "I do" on a day of joyful celebration. But, at his suggestion, we said, "I will," looking toward the future, not knowing what that future would bring. Before our wedding we were each free to change our minds and go our separate ways if things didn't go well between us. But from that day forward, we were obligated to work out our problems.

We promised that in our wedding vows, and it's been an important part of our journey through life together.

"...for better or worse, for richer or poorer..."

This is the part that so many couples fail to keep in mind during periods of disillusionment and when the going gets rough. Barb remembers:

> During our engagement we playfully repeated this part of the vow to each other – "for better or worse, but mostly for better; for richer or poorer, but mostly for richer." We joked and laughed about it, but that's what I assumed our life would be like – the "better" and the "richer."

> But life isn't always that way. I remember a time, during our school days, after our two daughters were born, when we had just $20 left for food and expenses for the four of us, to last us three weeks. Hmmm. Where was the "richer"?

> And we've surely had more than our share of the "better," but we've also had a taste of the "worse," such as when we moved into our new home bare dirt front and back. With two small children, we were eager to get the lawns in and fences up as soon as possible. But Bob broke his ankle right off the bat and couldn't do any of that kind of work for several weeks. Where was the "better" when we needed it?

We all need to keep in mind that accidents and tragedies, too, are a part of life, and they don't always happen to the other guy.

Sometimes even a joyful occasion can bring on a period of "worse," instead of "better." The birth of a child brings joy – but we might go through a rough period of adjustment to the new addition, especially if it's a first child. A raise or an extra bonus is certainly part of the "better," but if we disagree on how to use it, it can easily become a part of the "worse."

This type of thing will very likely continue to be a part of our life, too, and these are the very times that our unity as a couple can help us. We can rise above the "worse" and the "poorer" in life because we have each other and the love we share.

"...in sickness and in health..."

Again, most of us probably assume health. But what if our health fails, either physical or mental health? What if one of us becomes over-involved with alcohol or drugs? Or if sometime over the years one of us has a permanently disabling accident or stroke or some other disease? Does that count? Any of these can be life-changing events, and that isn't what we planned. Is that part of this vow? You bet it is! It might seem to be the hardest part to stick to but it's something to keep in mind before we make this commitment. There's no guarantee that the river of life will flow smoothly. It's a risk we take when we enter marriage. But what a noble thing it is to make this promise realizing that the risk is there!

"...to love and to cherish..."

This is Barb's favorite part of the vow:

> These words are my promise to Bob to always and ever keep him the center person of my life, the focus of my love, my Number 1 priority. And they're my assurance that he'll always cherish me in the same way.

> I feel confident and jubilant, knowing that he is and always will be there when I have joys to share and sorrows to bear. He's my confidante, my lover, my friend. He provides for me what no one else in the world can. And knowing that not only sustains me but reinforces my desire to keep *my* promise to him.

And Bob adds:

> I know that if I keep this part of my promise to Barb, all the other parts will be included. She's been the most important person in my life for decades, and I do love her and I do cherish her. She's precious to me beyond measure. Loving and cherishing imply to me not just a statement of the situation, but rather action.

Positive, loving words and deeds on my part let Barb know that my love for her is still strong.

I think loving and cherishing is what people want most in their marriage. To have it is truly a great blessing. How good it is to know that Barb loves me and cherishes me. It brings me warmth and security for today and for the future.

"…'til death us do part…"

This phrase points out the two sides of the vow– the permanence of marriage versus the reality of death. This is a difficult area to even think about, whether you're newly married or have had many years together. (We don't want to part from each other any more than the two of you do!) But we encourage you to share your thoughts and fears of each other's death. Bob tells us:

> My own death is easy enough to accept, intellectually. I'm ready any time God is. But I really don't like to think about how Barb will manage after I die. She *will* manage, I know that. But I don't like to think of the pain of my loss, and the loneliness that's bound to be a part of her life, at least for a while.
>
> When I think of her dying *before* I do, the pain and loneliness seem even greater. And yet I know how fortunate I am, how fortunate we both are to have had each other for even this long, and to have had the wonderful relationship that we've had. Many people live their whole lives without ever knowing the joy that can come from the deep intimacy of marriage. I know that, but knowing it won't make her death any easier. The feelings of sorrow and fear are real.

"…according to God's holy ordinance…"

This part of the vow refers to some of the things we mentioned earlier when we talked about God's plan for our marriage, things like living in unconditional love, and that marriage is a 100-100 proposition. In Matthew 19:4-6 God's holy ordinance is very clear:

Jesus said, "...he who made them from the beginning made them male and female, and said, 'For this reason a man shall leave his father and mother and be joined to his wife, and the two shall become one'. So they are no longer two but one. What therefore God has joined together, let no man put asunder."

This is God's holy ordinance. Read it again. This is how we, each of us, promised to live our lives. The promise was *our choice.*

"...and thereto I plight thee my troth."

These days this is often said as "and therefore I pledge you my love and faithfulness" but both phrases mean the same thing. Troth means faithfulness, loyalty, fidelity and to plight is to solemnly pledge. This part of the vow is a spoken statement of the decision to love and be faithful.

And Here Is Betrothal

So, those are the traditional wedding vows, and what they mean. At least, as they were explained to *us.* Now you're probably wondering just exactly what is a betrothal – and did you make one without even realizing it? Probably not.

Betrothal is an old term, familiar from the Christmas story in Luke 2, where Mary and Joseph were betrothed. In those days it was a fully-pledged commitment of faithfulness and fidelity, a pledge to wed, a pledge broken only by divorce. The English word is based on an ancient French word which means "to tell the truth." And of course that's what we've been urging you to do all through the exercises in this book.

To make a betrothal, a pledge of truth and faithfulness, infers that we want more than just that legal contract to seal our relationship. Our betrothal is a spiritual pledge, inviting God to become a part of our commitment to each other. It's so much easier to keep the commitment if we have God's help. We continually strive to keep Him an important part of our marriage, making it more than merely the convenient arrangement mentioned earlier.

We know from experience that our marriage can be much more than that legal contract. Even if Christianity is foreign to you, if you've never belonged to a church, if you've never asked God to be a part of your life, ever before, we urge you to try it now. Ask God to help you with your marriage, to be a partner with the two of you.

We want a living and growing marriage, with God at the center. We want Him to be with us every day as we reach out to each other in love, and to be there for us when we need Him. We want Him to be with us on those days when it's easy to love, and to be by our side to give us strength at those times when it's maybe *not* so easy to make the decision to love. This is what makes a Christian marriage so different and unique, compared to a secular marriage. It has a spiritual quality to it.

It doesn't happen automatically, though, just because we *want* it; there are many temptations and distractions in our path. God promises to help us with those temptations, in 1 Corinthians 10:13, but we have to continually strive to keep God in our marriage so that He *can* help us resist the temptations.

Engagement as Contrasted with Betrothal

Let's take a minute to tell you a little about our engagement. Barb likes to talk about that:

> It was a beautiful time in our lives, much as yours probably is right now. Since we were paying for our own wedding, we did most of the planning for it. And since we didn't have a whole lot of money to work with, we shopped for the best bargains, and that meant a *lot* of shopping! We spent most of our free time together, looking at wedding cakes, gifts for ushers and brides-maids, invitations, flowers, and all the other things that go along with wedding preparations. I felt very special. Everyone seemed to care about us – the florist, the dressmaker, our families and friends. They all wanted our event to be a memorable one.

There wasn't anything extraordinary there, just the normal activities for an engagement period.

That's engagement. So what's betrothal? A betrothal establishes a relationship that is finalized and celebrated at the wedding. A betrothal deepens and expands the engagement; a wedding deepens the betrothal and celebrates the permanence of the relationship. Betrothal is taking the step, before the marriage begins, into a commitment of faithfulness and fidelity. God uses this time to prepare us for our marriage; *we've* experienced that. Bob tells about our betrothal:

> With all the love and support we had, and all the activity involved in those pre-wedding days, we seldom took time to ponder the seriousness of this step. We didn't actually make a formal betrothal – we simply decided to get married. We did agree that it was to last for a lifetime; we were both committed to that. We just weren't sure *how* to make it last; our betrothal was incomplete.

Barb adds:

> Looking back on it, I can see that during this time of wedding preparations we were learning more and more about each other, how we each come to decisions, how to make them together, how we each behaved when we didn't get our own way, how we each reacted when we found the perfect top decoration for our cake, and so on. It was actually a time of preparation for our *marriage* as well as for our *wedding*. But at the time, our attention was focused on the social aspects of the wedding – making sure that all the "required" things were taken care of, like the flowers, minister, church, and all the rest. And getting the invitations out on the proper day – not too soon, not too late – all those things that we've realized in the long run are really not that important. Those things don't guarantee a long and successful married life. They don't even contribute to it. The only thing they do is maybe prevent it from ever getting started, because we can't agree on some part of it!

To say that we are engaged puts the wedding plans in motion. Engagement suggests activities: we think about the church, the invitations, the cake, the flowers, and on and on. But betrothal sets the *marriage*, the psychological union, in motion. It's our pledge to love each other fully, a profound declaration of the *relationship* between a woman and a man. (Note that a betrothal, as important and meaningful as it is, only sets the marriage in motion; it's the wedding ceremony, "before God and these witnesses," that gives the marriage the finality it needs.)

Making a Betrothal Pledge

These days, of course, many couples don't bother with a betrothal, or even know about it. They get right into the engagement activities and on to the wedding plans. (Maybe if they took the time for a betrothal the divorce rate wouldn't be as high as it is.) But at the end of this section *you* will each have an opportunity to write a betrothal pledge. We suggest that as you write you keep in mind the ideas that we've just presented to you – things like what the traditional wedding vow really means, and what a betrothal is and what it's for. We want to impress on you the value and the significance of taking the time to *write* a betrothal pledge. It's likely that your wedding vows may be more meaningful because now you've heard the explanation and you might have already begun to live out your betrothal commitment.

Writing a betrothal pledge is an important and serious step. This is a conscious, life-long commitment being considered here. Your commitment so far has been only oral, if you're like most engaged couples. Even a pre-nuptial agreement usually involves only property; it doesn't mention the commitment involved in a marriage.

Realize that writing a betrothal, even though it isn't legally binding, may be the beginning of a new dimension in your relationship, and it will probably make a difference in your lives. This is when you carefully and clearly state your truthful intentions in writing, and sign your name to it. During your wedding, then, you'll make a public affirmation before God and your friends of the vows and intentions you've already stated privately to each other today. (But the words will be different.) Written with sincerity, the private vow can be as important to you as the publicly-stated vow.

Or...

Now is truly a time for a life-giving decision, unselfish on your part, and giving life to your fiancé in the promise of life-long love. Think carefully about it. We know this is a busy time for you, with all the wedding preparations – we remember how hectic it was for us. But it's important that you take a moment during this busy time to assess where you are with yourself, and where you are with each other. Is this marriage, at this time, what's best for both of you? Is this what God would choose for you to do? Now is the time to honestly evaluate where you are in your relationship with each other. We urge you to take the time to evaluate your feelings of readiness for marriage – readiness for marriage to this person, at this time.

Consider the pressures of family and friends to go ahead with the plans already made, reminding you of the money already spent. Do you feel pressure? Are you being swept up in the excitement of wedding preparations without giving enough serious thought to the marriage that will follow? Perhaps you're feeling social pressure to marry now that you've found someone who's willing to marry you, knowing the possibility that you may never get another chance? Have you been looking for an opportunity to postpone or to cancel your wedding, but the time never seemed quite right? Are you settling for "peace at any price"?

We aren't trying to scare you. We just don't want you to do anything you might not be ready for. Only *you* can judge that. Be honest about your feelings and your thoughts. If for any reason you *cannot* make a deeper commitment just now, please be honest with yourself and with each other. Tell your fiancé your reasons for feeling as you do. You surely won't be the first to postpone or cancel wedding plans. Couples may love each other very deeply and yet not be ready for marriage, or realize that they need more time to work on their relationship with each other. If that's the case, please tell your fiancé what you're thinking and feeling. Use this writing and discussion time to tell why you can't make a betrothal pledge just now.

Suggestions For Getting Started

We know that it can be difficult to get started on a betrothal pledge – it was for each of us, and we'd been married a long time before we actually put it down on paper. But we'll give you a few opening sentences to help you get started. For example, you could start by answering the question "How do I plan to love you and what does your love mean to me?" Or begin with "I want to live the rest of my life with you because..." and go on from there. Or start with your own phrase, one that comes from your heart.

This time we encourage you to put your thoughts in the form of a love-letter, to make it even more special – this may be the truest and most meaningful love-letter you've every written. And when it comes time to share your writing, we suggest that you each read your own letter to your fiancé, rather than exchanging notebooks as you've been doing. Incidentally, we still write letters like this occasionally, renewing our commitment to each other. This written expression of our love is as special to us, after all our years together, as it is to you. The vows and promises we've made to each other have become more real and taken on deeper meaning as we've grown together during our marriage. They've become another source of great joy.

SUMMARY

You've read the traditional marriage vow, and the meaning of each phrase it contains. You've learned what a betrothal is and that engagement puts the wedding in motion, while betrothal puts the marriage in motion. We've asked you to seriously consider your readiness for marriage, and to be honest with your fiancé if you feel that the time is not right. We've even given you suggestions for getting started.

So, with all that, plus the groundwork you've done, you are now ready to write a betrothal of your own. Or explain to your fiancé why you can't. Either is okay.

An additional note from Bob:

> At a time like this, it can be difficult for some, especially the guys, to express true feelings – we're afraid of getting emotional and think we have to keep up that macho image. Well, try to get past that. We need to, so that we can share our deepest feelings, and our greatest love. This is a very important time and if the emotions want to come to the surface, let them. It's your inner-most self coming out and you should share that with each other, not try to hide it. It's part of *you*. This is a special time in your relationship and it calls for true openness.

You'll have plenty of time to write, time for probably two full pages in your notebook, so don't rush. Write what you need to write. But if you do finish quickly, still wait until you hear the signal to stop writing; this is one time for sure you don't want to interrupt your fiancé before he/she is finished.

Reflections on Betrothal

(Minimum writing time 30 minutes, discussion time 15 minutes)

The love-letter you'll write for your betrothal should come from your heart, of course. But if you have trouble getting started, you might try using one of the following starters:

- To me, marrying you means…
- I plan to deepen our relationship by…
- To me, your love means…

Or complete one of these sentences:

- The love between us today will not die because…
- I want to live the rest of my life with you because…
- I plan to make ours a Christian marriage by…

Or perhaps:

- I cannot make a betrothal pledge to you at this time because…

Or write your own, one that comes from your heart.

(Remember to write in the form of a love-letter)

"To love and be loved is the greatest joy on earth!"

– Anonymous

13

The Happy Ending
Leading to a New Beginning

Now that you've finished with the exercises at the end of each chapter, we urge you to go over each page of "Reflections" again, writing a second time or completing any you didn't answer for whatever reason. You might have decided at the time that the particular question didn't apply to you and now it does, or that you had already answered it, or whatever. But now that you've finished all of them, you're different people – you've each learned new things about your fiancé and have clarified some of the things you knew before. This review of the questions will allow you to cover items that perhaps one or both of you had glossed over the first time through. It won't take as long as the first time, of course, but will be well worth the effort.

If You've Decided Not To Marry

If either or both of you have decided that marriage wouldn't work for you at this time, you can stay together as friends or part as friends. Appreciate the pleasure and joy that you've brought each other, and realize that not just *any* man can pair up with just *any* woman to make a successful union. Both people have to want it, and both must be willing to make the compromises and sacrifices necessary for a lasting marriage. If the two of you don't have that, find comfort in the fact that you've learned it before your wedding, before starting a family. Wish each other well, and move on in your life.

Or You've Decided To Postpone...

Having made the difficult decision to postpone your wedding, we encourage you to spend whatever time is necessary to work through the problems that have come to the surface. Remember that not all problems *can* be resolved, but perhaps you can work out those causing you the most concern. Go over the Reflection sheet again. If you find that you still have areas or specific topics that aren't the way you think they should be, get a good book or two on making marriage work. There are many available, both in regular book stores and in Christian book stores. Often, a different author can phrase things in such a way as to make more sense for you. You might also want to seek additional pastoral counseling. Remember, though, it's possible that God has other plans for you at this time.

And Now...

For those of you who have decided to continue with your wedding plans, we have one final exercise for you, a short ceremony. For this you will need a new candle in a nice candle holder (a 6" taper will do, but it can be taller if that's what you have), a Bible, your betrothal pledges (from chapter 12), privacy, and the following page (or a photocopy of it).

(Put this guidebook down now, while you get those items.)

A Private Ceremony

Begin with a short prayer, asking God to be with you at this time. (If you aren't Christian, we urge you to try this anyway; you'll like it.)

Then:

- Light the candle
- One of you read aloud the following:
  - ▸ A candle is analogous to the love of Christ, who said, "I am the Light of the world" (John 8:12).
  - ▸ As a candle brightens the darkness, so does love illuminate one's life.
  - ▸ As a candle gives warmth, so does love.
  - ▸ As a candle gives a sense of direction and draws people together, so does love.
  - ▸ As a candle burns, the wax melting on the candle disfigures the candle. So also a love relationship involves elements of risk and pain.
  - ▸ Notice that a candle, in order to fulfill itself, must expend itself, or burn itself out. If it is never lit, it is never fulfilled, and its purpose for being is limited and empty.
  - ▸ So, too, love must totally give of itself for the other for it's purpose to be fulfilled.
- Read 1 Corinthians 13:4-13, and 1 John 4:7-12.
- Together say a prayer, for whatever you choose to ask of God in your marriage. Keep in mind the many topics covered during this marriage preparation time, noting areas where, either as a couple or individually, you will be needing help.
- Holding hands, you might want to read aloud to each other your betrothal love-letter.
- Then, if you choose to, each repeat the following formal betrothal:

▶ I pledge to you _____ my love,
faithfulness, and devotion as long as we both shall live.

This will not be a legal union, of course, but it is a true promise of your commitment.

- Close the ceremony with The Lord's Prayer:
  Our Father, who art in heaven,
  Hallowed be thy name.
  Thy kingdom come. Thy will be done,
  On earth as it is in heaven.
  Give us this day our daily bread
  And forgive us our trespasses
  as we forgive those who trespass against us.
  Lead us not into temptation, but deliver us from evil.
  For Thine is the kingdom,
  and the power and the glory,
  Forever and ever. Amen.

(Remember to blow out the candle)

You might choose, as many couples do, to use this very candle in your wedding ceremony, a Unity candle which has already fulfilled a part of its job.

We wish you the best in your married life together.

About the Authors

Bob and Barbara Hickman have been involved with helping couples enjoy and appreciate their marriage relationship for over 20 years. They believe that their strongest qualification for helping these couples is their own long-term, satisfying marriage, along with the information gleaned from reading numerous books on how to make a marriage life-long, happy, and fulfilling.

They first became actively involved in helping couples shortly after their first Marriage Encounter weekend. Less than a year later they added extensive involvement in Engaged Encounter, with the objective of assuring the existence of a marriage preparation program for their own teenage daughters when the time came.

For many years they were a presenting couple for both Marriage Encounter and Engaged Encounter. They also established and served as president of Lutheran Engaged Encounter of Northern California and served as president of Lutheran Engaged Encounter International. This led them to create a one-day workshop called One In Christ for engaged and newly married couples unable to attend a full weekend program.

Bob and Barb were inspired to write this book when they were approached by a friend whose daughter, living in Madagascar, was about to be married and had no opportunity for pre-marital counseling of any kind. Since then it has been praised by a number of reviewers and publishers and used by both engaged and newly married couples. This up-dated edition, the first offered to the general public, was at the request of yet another engaged couple.

Bob has a Ph.D. in Chemical Engineering. He worked as a research scientist and manager and is now retired and an active community volunteer. Barb has a B.A. and an M.A. both in Speech Communication and has had additional training and experience in family, marriage, and pre-marriage counseling. She is currently offers workshops in public speaking and hosts a local weekly television talk show. She is also creating a series of books on public speaking for children. They have two married daughters and four grandchildren.

Index

"We are each of us angels with only one wing. And we can only fly by embracing each other."

— Luciano de Cresenzo

Quick Order Form

Publishing

(Make a photocopy of this form)

Fax orders   **(925) 447-2053**
    (Send a photocopy of the completed form with credit card information and signature.)

Telephone orders: **(925) 447-2053** (Have your credit card ready.)

E-mail orders: **www.bigoakpublishing.com**

Mail orders: **Big Oak Publishing**
                   2265 Sherry Court #101
                   Livermore, CA 94550

Name_____Date_____

Address_____

City_____State_____Zip_____

Telephone_____E-mail_____

Please send ___ copies of *Prepare for Your Marriage: A Guidebook for Engaged Couples* @ $16.95 plus $4.00 for shipping. (Please add 8.25% for products shipped to California addresses.) I understand that I may return it for a full refund, for any reason.

         ___ Books @ $16.95   _____
         Shipping @ $4.00 per book   _____
         8.25% Tax (California only)   _____
         Total remittance   _____

☐   Check enclosed

☐   Credit card (circle one)   Visa   MasterCard

Card number_____Expiration date_____

Name on card_____

Authorized signature _____

Allow 4-6 weeks for shipping